WOMEN AND THE LAW

REPRINTED

FROM THE

2007 ANNUAL REPORT

OF THE

CONGRESSIONAL-EXECUTIVE
COMMISSION ON CHINA

ONE HUNDRED TENTH CONGRESS

FIRST SESSION

OCTOBER 10, 2007

Printed for the use of the Congressional-Executive Commission on China

Available via the World Wide Web: http://www.cecc.gov

U.S. GOVERNMENT PRINTING OFFICE

40–784 PDF   WASHINGTON : 2007

For sale by the Superintendent of Documents, U.S. Government Printing Office
Internet: bookstore.gpo.gov   Phone: toll free (866) 512–1800; DC area (202) 512–1800
Fax: (202) 512–2104   Mail: Stop IDCC, Washington, DC 20402–0001

CONTENTS

STATUS OF WOMEN

INTRODUCTION

The Commission has noted in the past that the Chinese government has been more vigorous in publicizing and condemning abuse against women than in other areas concerning human rights.[1] In 2003, 2004, and 2006, the Commission observed that, while China had built an expansive legal framework to protect women's rights and interests, loopholes and inadequate implementation remained that left women vulnerable to widespread abuse, discrimination, and harassment at home and in the workplace.[2] The Commission noted in 2004–2006 that China's economic reforms have increased opportunities for women to build their own businesses, but these reforms still leave many women, when compared to men, with fewer employment opportunities, less earning power, less access to education, especially in rural areas, and increasing risks from HIV/AIDS.[3] In its 2004–2006 Annual Reports, the Commission also noted the existence of women's organizations that advocate on behalf of women's rights within the confines of government and Communist Party policy.[4] In its 2005 Annual Report, the Commission observed that China's Constitution and laws provide for the equal rights of women, but, as noted in 2006, vague language and inadequate implementation continue to hinder the effectiveness of legal protections written in the Constitution and national laws.[5]

LAWS AND INSTITUTIONS

The Chinese Constitution and laws provide for the equal rights of women.[6] In addition, the Program for the Development of Chinese Women seeks to increase women's development by 2010 in areas of the economy, decisionmaking and management, education, health, law, and the environment.[7] CECC Annual Reports dating from 2003 have noted that the number of laws and regulations promoting the equal rights of women has expanded, with a noticeable difference after 2004.

In August 2005, the National People's Congress (NPC) Standing Committee passed an amendment to the Law on the Protection of Women's Rights and Interests (LPWRI), which prohibit sexual harassment and domestic violence, and require government entities at all levels to give women assistance to assert their rights in court.[8] At least nine provincial and municipal governments have passed regulations to strengthen the implementation of the LPWRI.[9] For example, Shanghai's regulations, passed in April 2007, explicitly prohibit five types of sexual harassment, namely verbal, written, pictorial, electronic transmission of information such as text messaging, and physical sexual harassment.[10] The 2002–2004 Annual Reports noted that although there was initially no specific law on sexual harassment, people began to file sexual harassment cases in court and several women won lawsuits against their employers, in part due to greater economic openness and government and women's organizations' efforts to build awareness.[11] In addition, at least 15 provincial and municipal governments have detailed domestic violence regulations, and the Ministry of Public Security and the All-China Women's Federation (ACWF), among others, issued guidelines in 2007 that will legally obligate police officers to respond immediately to domestic violence calls and to assist domestic violence victims, or face punishment.[12]

Previous annual reports have noted that the lack of a national definition on key terms, such as discrimination against women and sexual harassment, hinder effective implementation of the amended LPWRI and other policy instruments.[13] In addition, even though the amended Marriage Law of 2001 and the amended LPWRI prohibit domestic violence, "domestic violence" is not defined, and case rulings in domestic violence cases are inconsistent due to the lack of clear standards in laws and judicial explanations.[14] Other hurdles in accessing justice include domestic violence victims bearing the burden in bringing complaints, lack of detailed provisions on how to implement policy measures, and limited public understanding and awareness, among other factors.[15] Recent surveys show that domestic violence and sexual harassment remain widespread. For example, 30 percent of Chinese families experience domestic violence, and 74.8 percent of female migrant workers engaged in the service industry in Changsha city report experiencing some form of verbal or physical sexual harassment.[16]

GENDER DISPARITIES

Economy

China's transition to a market economy has had contradictory influences on the social status of women, who contribute to over 40 percent of China's gross domestic product, offering them both "greater freedom and mobility," and "greater threats . . . at home and in the workplace."[17] The Commission's 2003 Annual Report notes that women workers face particular hardships in finding a job, as they are often the first to be fired and the last to be hired, and there exists weak labor protection measures, inadequate maternity insurance, unequal compensation and benefits when compared to men for equal work, and fewer opportunities for advancement, among other factors.[18] There are also concerns that women's participation in the economy is unevenly distributed between rural and urban areas, and that the market transition has increased fees in rural areas, impoverishing some families and harming girls' access to education.[19] Young women are increasingly migrating to urban areas to find work, leaving them vulnerable to trafficking, forced labor, and other abuses.[20]

At the same time, some women are succeeding as entrepreneurs in China, in certain measures even in comparison to men.[21] For example, most of these women entrepreneurs work in small and medium-sized companies, accounting for 20 percent of the total number of entrepreneurs in China. Among them, 60 percent have become successful in the past decade and 95 percent of the companies that they run have been very successful. These companies have created more job opportunities for women as well, since 60 percent of the staff tends to be women.[22] [See Section II—Worker Rights.]

Decisionmaking and Management

Women account for 40 percent of government positions, yet this number may be misleading as very few hold positions with decisionmaking power. For example, the Ministry of Civil Affairs estimates that less than 1 percent of village committees and village-level Communist Party Committees in China's 653,000 administrative villages were headed by women in 2004. In March 2007, the NPC announced that female representatives should account for at least 22 percent of the seats in the 11th NPC, with representatives to be elected by the end of January 2008, and at least 30 percent of civil servant posts must be held by women.[23] Various provincial and municipal governments have also announced gender quotas for positions in their local governments and local people's congresses.[24]

HIV/AIDS and Health

Chinese health statistics over the past five years continue to reflect women's disadvantaged status, and also reflect central and local governments' slow pace in effectively addressing health issues that are known to disparately impact women, especially women in rural areas. The Commission's 2005 Annual Report noted that women make up an increasingly larger percentage of newly reported HIV/AIDS cases, an observation confirmed by official Chinese government news media.[25] This trend has continued in the 2006–2007 reporting period,[26] although the government has taken some steps to increase HIV/AIDS awareness among women used in prostitution.[27] Although the Commission's 2003 Annual Report observed that China had not taken the necessary initiatives to increase awareness among this group, these recent steps suggest a possible positive development if they are implemented effectively.[28]

China is the only country in the world where the rate of suicide is higher among women than among men.[29] According to the editor of China Women's News, 157,000 women commit suicide each year in China, 25 percent more than men. In rural areas, the instance of suicide among women is three to four times higher than the instance among men, and three to five times higher than the instance among women who live in urban areas. Domestic violence is the main cause of suicide among women in rural areas.[30] While there has been a decline in maternal mortality rates since 1991, there is a widening gap between urban and rural areas, with women in rural areas experiencing significantly higher mortality rates when compared with maternal mortality rates in urban areas and the national average.[31] Moreover, rural women's rates of illnesses are 5 percent higher when compared with rural men's rates of illnesses, most likely as a result of long working hours, poor nutrition and care after childbirth, and the collapse of the rural cooperative medical system.[32] [See Section II—Health.]

Access to Education, Especially in Rural Areas

Women continue to have less access to education in rural areas and lower educational levels when compared to men, although women's organizations and the government have initiated programs in recent years to reverse this trend by providing economic incentives to send girls to school or seeking to change traditional rural attitudes that give preference to the education of sons. Despite 99 percent enrollment rates for girls and boys, only 43 percent of girls in rural areas, as compared with 61 percent of boys, complete education higher than junior middle school.[33] Furthermore, the National Bureau of Statistics released statistical data in 2006 showing that more than 70 percent of those who are illiterate and 15 years of age and older are women, a figure that has increased since 2001.[34] In an attempt to address these issues in part, government and government-affiliated organizations have organized local-level "Spring Bud" programs that aim to help girls stay in school around the country.[35]

Rural Land Reallocation and the Rights of "Married-Out Women"

"Married-out women" in rural areas continue to experience violation of their land and property rights, although judges have recently ruled in favor of women in certain types of lawsuits, and some provinces are issuing regulations that seek to strengthen implementation of existing legal protections. Village committees, when determining who should be eligible to receive shares of collectively owned land assets, may order decisions that legitimize discrimination against "married-out women." "Married-out women" include women who have either married men from other villages, but whose household registration (*hukou*) remains in their birthplace, whose *hukou* is transferred from one place back to their birthplace, or whose *hukou* is transferred to their husbands' village.

These women are especially vulnerable to violation of their rights, including rights to use land, to receive compensation for the land, to use the land for residential purposes, and to have access to collective welfare resources.[36] Legal protections in the form of the PRC Law on Land Contract in Rural Areas, the Marriage Law, and other laws, guarantee women the same land rights as men. Judges have ruled in favor of women in four lawsuits concerning land rights since August 2005, and there have been reports of other successful cases within the last two years.[37] Most of these women who have won lawsuits, however, have been those who still live in their villages after marrying men from other villages.[38]

There are still tremendous difficulties for "married-out women" to use legal channels to seek redress for violations of their rights. For example, lawyers have noted that the LPWRI and relevant regulations in Guangdong province guarantee the property rights of women, but they lack detailed articles that could be used to protect these rights.[39] In addition, each village also has its own set of laws, which according to the PRC Organic Law of Village Committees (Organic Law) should not contravene national laws and regulations.[40] Yet the Organic Law does not indicate how to prevent or resolve this disconnect, with the consequence that some villages uphold their own laws even when they are in conflict with the

LPWRI and other laws.[41] In May 2007, Guangdong province passed regulations to strengthen its implementation of the LPWRI, with the rule that neither organizations, such as the village committee, nor individuals can prevent or force rural women to change their *hukou* as a result of marriage, divorce, or widowhood.[42] In addition, the regulations state that village rules, laws, and resolutions concerning land rights must not violate women's rights on the basis of marriage, divorce, or widowhood.[43]

WOMEN'S ORGANIZATIONS

Women's organizations have been particularly active in the last few years, although these groups advocate on behalf of women's rights within the confines of government and Communist Party policy. The All-China Women's Federation (ACWF), a Communist Party-led mass organization, plays a supporting role in the formation of some of these organizations while others operate more independently and sometimes with unregistered status.[44] There were 2,000 active organizations by 1989, and the Fourth World Conference on Women in 1995 helped to launch other women's organizations, such as the Center for Women's Law Studies and Legal Services of Peking University and the Maple Women's Psychological Counseling Center. In addition, several women leaders jointly founded the advocacy project Women's Watch—China in April 2005.

Within the last year, the China Women's University established a legal center for women and children, and there have been various seminars and workshops sponsored by universities, lawyers' associations, and local women's federations to raise awareness of women's issues among lawyers, judges, public officials, and academics.[45] The ACWF works with the Chinese government to support women's rights, implement programs for disadvantaged women, and provide a limited measure of legal counseling and training for women.[46] As a Party organization, however, the ACWF does not promote women's interests when such interests conflict with Party policies that limit women's rights. For example, in 2005, an ACWF representative in Yunnan province refused to allow a leading women's rights activist to represent over 500 women in Yunnan in seeking redress for lost land, on the grounds that such interference could "influence stability."[47] In addition, the ACWF has been silent about the abuses of Chinese government population planning policies and remains complicit in the coercive enforcement of birth limits.[48]

NON-DISCRIMINATION IN EMPLOYMENT AND THE WORKPLACE

Women account for 60 percent of total rural laborers, and by the end of 2004, there were 337 million women working in cities and rural areas, which accounted for 44.8 percent of the total workforce, roughly women's proportion of China's general population.[49] Women still face tremendous challenges in the workplace, and women migrant workers face particular hardship. For example, more than 70 percent of women in a 2007 survey reported worrying about losing their jobs after becoming pregnant, and there have been numerous cases of women dismissed after they became pregnant.[50] In addition, a 2006 survey of women migrant workers conducted by the ACWF found that only 6.7 percent of surveyed workers had maternity insurance. Of the 36.4 percent who reported that they were allowed to take maternity leave, 64.5 percent said this leave was unpaid.[51] Some local governments have established programs to provide loans, training, and legal aid for woman workers.[52] For example, the legal aid center in Jinan city provides legal services for migrant women workers.[53] The ACWF also has programs such as the Two Million Project, launched in 2003, which aims to train 2 million laid-off women so that they can find reemployment.[54] [See Section II—Worker Rights.]

CONTINUING CHALLENGES IN THE WORKPLACE

The Chinese government has passed a substantial body of protective legislation, particularly in the area of labor laws and regulations. For example, the 1978 Temporary Measures on Providing for Old, Weak, Sick, and Handicapped Cadres (Temporary Measures) require women to retire at 55, and men at 60.[55] Chinese academics and government officials have noted that the Temporary Measures discriminate against women.[56] In addition, requirements for employment based on height, weight, gender, age, and beauty are not uncommon. In 2006, a transportation company based in Hubei province issued rules stipulating that female attendants must stay within certain height and weight requirements, and that attendants whose weight exceeded 60 kilograms (132 pounds) would be laid off.[57] Despite some legal protections, both urban and rural women in China continue to have limited earning power when compared to men, and women lag behind men in finding employment in higher-wage urban areas.[58]

POPULATION PLANNING

INTRODUCTION

During the past five years, the Chinese government has maintained population planning policies that violate international human rights standards. As this Commission noted in 2006, "The Chinese government strictly controls the reproductive lives of Chinese women. Since the early 1980s, the government's population planning policy has limited most women in urban areas to bearing one child, while permitting many women in rural China to bear a second child if their first child is female. Officials have coerced compliance with the policy through a system marked by pervasive propaganda, mandatory monitoring of women's reproductive cycles, mandatory contraception, mandatory birth permits, coercive fines for failure to comply, and, in some cases, forced sterilization and abortion. The Chinese government's population planning laws and regulations contravene international human rights standards by limiting the number of children that women may bear, by coercing compliance with population targets through heavy fines, and by discriminating against 'out-of-plan' children."[1]

As this Commission reported in 2005 and 2006, China's population planning policies in both their nature and implementation constitute human rights violations according to international standards. During 2007, human rights abuses related to China's population planning policies clearly were not limited to physically coerced abortions. Local officials have violated Chinese law by punishing citizens, such as imprisoned legal advocate Chen Guangcheng, who have drawn attention to population planning abuses by government officials. Moreover, as described below, population planning policies have exacerbated imbalanced sex ratios—a male to female ratio of 118:100, according to the U.S. Department of State, but reportedly higher in some localities and for second births.

OVERVIEW OF RECENT DEVELOPMENTS

China's population planning policies exert government control over women's reproductive lives, impose punitive measures against citizens not in compliance with the population planning policies, and engender additional abuses by officials who implement the policies at local levels. The government states that population planning policies have prevented more than 300 million births since implementation, and it justifies continuing the policies to maintain controls over population growth.[2] In 2002, when the Chinese government codified its population planning policies into national law, an official stated that China "does not yet possess the conditions for a relaxation of [the] birth policy, but there is also no need to tighten it."[3] A decision issued by the Communist Party Central Committee and State Council in December 2006 promoted the continuation of basic national policies on population planning.[4] In July 2007, the head of the Population and Family Planning Commission reiterated that the policies would remain in place.[5]

China's population planning policies deny Chinese women control over their reproductive lives. The Population and Family Planning Law and related local regulations permit women to bear one child, with limited exceptions.[6] Women who bear "out-of-plan" children face, along with their family members, harsh economic penalties in the form of "social compensation fees" that can range to multiples of a locality's yearly average income.[7] Authorities also subject citizens who violate population planning rules to demotions or loss of jobs and other punitive measures.[8] Authorities have used legal action and coercive measures to collect money from poor citizens who cannot afford to pay the fees.[9] The fees entrench the disparity between rich and poor, as wealthier citizens have come to view paying the fees as a way to buy out of population planning restrictions.[10] Public officials also have been able to flaunt restrictions. Official Chinese media reported in 2007 that the Hunan province family planning commission found that from 2000 to 2005, nearly 2,000 officials in the province had violated the Population and Family Planning Law.[11] In September 2007, the government and Party announced new measures to monitor public officials' adherence to population planning policies and deny promotions to officials who violate them.[12] In recent years, the government has introduced more programs to reward citizens' compliance with family planning policies, but it has retained punitive measures.[13] In May 2007, the national Population and Family Planning Commission adopted a plan to "rectify" out-of-plan births in urban parts of China.[14] Controls imposed on Chinese women and their families, and additional abuses engendered by the system, from forced abortion to discriminatory policies against "out-of-plan" children, violate standards in the Convention on the Elimination of All Forms of Discrimination Against Women,[15] Convention on the Rights of the Child,[16] and the International Covenant on Economic, Social, and Cultural Rights,[17] the terms of which China is bound to uphold as a state party to these treaties.

Abuses in the enforcement of population planning policies have further eroded citizens' rights. Although the Population and Family Planning Law provides for punishment of officials who violate citizens' rights in promoting compliance,[18] reports from recent years indicate that abuses continue. Media reports in 2005 publicized abuses in Linyi, Shandong province, where officials enforced compliance through forced sterilizations, forced abortions, beatings, and other abuses.[19] Citizens who challenge government offenses continue to face harsh repercussions. After legal advocate Chen Guangcheng exposed abuses in Linyi, authorities launched a campaign of harassment against him that culminated in a four-year, three-month prison sentence imposed in 2006 and affirmed by a higher court in 2007.[20] [See also Section II—Rights of Criminal Suspects and Defendants for more information.] Structural incentives for local officials to coerce compliance exacerbate the potential for abuses. In spring 2007, local officials in Bobai county, Guangxi Zhuang Autonomous Region (GZAR), initiated a wide-scale campaign to control birthrates after the GZAR government reprimanded officials for failing to meet population targets. Officials reportedly required all women to submit to examinations and subjected women to fines, forced sterilization, and forced abortions. Authorities looted homes and seized possessions of citizens who did not pay the fines.[21] In May, Bobai residents rioted in protest of government abuses. Residents of Rong county, also in the GZAR, protested population planning policies later the same month.[22] In one potentially positive development, an intermediate court in Hebei province agreed in 2007 to hear a couple's lawsuit against a local family planning commission for a forced abortion seven years ago, reportedly the first time a court has taken an appeal in this type of case.[23]

The government has taken limited steps to address social problems exacerbated by population planning policies, such as unbalanced sex ratios[24] and decreasing social support for China's aging population. In 2006, the government announced that the following year it would extend across China a pilot project to provide financial support to rural parents with only one child or two girls, once the parents have reached 60 years of age.[25] The Communist Party Central Committee and State Council decision issued in 2006 describes the unbalanced sex ratio as "inevitably influencing social stability," advocates steps to address discrimination against girls and women, and promotes measures to stop sex-selective abortion.[26] Sex ratios stand at roughly 118 male births to 100 female births, with higher rates in some parts of the country and for second births. Demographers and population experts consider a normal male-female birth ratio to be between 103 to 107:100.[27]

In 2006, the National People's Congress Standing Committee considered, but decided not to pass, a proposed amendment to the Criminal Law that would have criminalized sex-selective abortion.[28] Local governments have instituted prohibitions against fetal sex-determination and sex-selective abortion. For example, in 2006, Henan province passed a regulation imposing financial penalties on these acts where they take place outside of limited approved parameters.[29]

At the same time the government has taken some steps to deal with the sex imbalance and discriminatory attitudes toward girls, some provincial governments have enforced policies that institutionalize biases against girls by permitting families to have a second child where the first child is a girl.[30] According to some observers, imbalanced sex ratios and a resulting shortage of marriage partners have already contributed to, or will exacerbate in the future, the problem of human trafficking.[31] [See Section II—Human Trafficking, and Section II—North Korean Refugees in China.]

Within individual provincial-level jurisdictions, a range of factors beyond birth rates affect local population growth. Internal migration has contributed to demographic shifts within ethnic minority autonomous regions, among other areas. In 2006, authorities in the Xinjiang Uighur Autonomous Region (XUAR) acknowledged that floating and migrant populations would continue to contribute to the region's high rate of population growth, but also announced the government would carry out its population planning policies by continuing measures to control birth rates. A series of articles from official media specifically indicated that the XUAR government would target impoverished ethnic minority areas as the focus of these measures.[32] [See Section II—Ethnic Minority Rights, and Section IV—Tibet, for more information on population issues in ethnic minority areas.]

During 2008, the Commission will continue to monitor and report on violations of international human rights standards in China related to forced abortions, social compensation fees, licensing for births, control of women's reproductive cycles, and all other issues.

HEALTH

MENTAL HEALTH

In December 2006, the Beijing Municipal People's Congress issued a new Regulation on Mental Health. On its face, the new regulation prohibits local police from arbitrarily detaining the city's mentally ill as Beijing prepares to host the 2008 Summer Olympic Games.[1] Under the new regulation, which went into effect in March 2007, public security officials may remove a mentally ill person to a mental health center only if that person "harms or poses a serious threat to public safety, a person's life, or property."[2] The precise meaning of these words and how they are to be interpreted remain unclear.

The new regulation requires that at least two mental health doctors make determinations of medical necessity for involuntary hospital admission. It also provides for review of involuntary admission by a review body. On these points the regulation is not dissimilar from the UN Principles for the Protection of Persons with Mental Illness and for the Improvement of Mental Health Care.[3] However, while the UN Principles provide that the review body complete its review "as soon as possible" and "in accordance with expeditious procedures," the Beijing regulation requires that the review be completed "within three months"—a period of time that could accomplish the purpose of removing persons from the streets for the duration of the 2008 Olympic Games (August 8–24, 2008) or longer, without violating the letter of the law.[4]

HIV/AIDS

Many international experts concur that over the past five years, the Chinese central government's policies to combat the spread of HIV/AIDS have, in general, progressively strengthened. On this issue of importance to China's leaders, however, the government's worries about uncontrolled citizen activism and foreign-affiliated nongovernmental organizations (NGOs) have limited their policies potential effectiveness. During its best periods, the government has developed a set of policies and laws and committed funding, and in limited but important ways engaged international groups and its own NGO community. China's HIV/AIDS policy has also demonstrated unusual openness to working with marginalized communities such as migrant workers, the homosexual community, women and men used in prostitution, and drug users. Due to these efforts and the increase in the use of anti-retroviral drugs, the death rate has reportedly decreased in recent years.[5]

China recorded its first AIDS case in 1989,[6] and by mid-2002, official Chinese government and UN figures estimated that between 1 million to 1.5 million people were infected with HIV.[7] Recent UN figures estimate there are about 650,000 people living with HIV in China today, but experts believe this estimate to be low on account of changes in estimation methodology and procedures.[8] While China is a country with a low prevalence of the disease nationwide, health experts say the disease is moving into the general population, with most new infections being spread sexually, followed by drug use.[9] China reported 18,543 new cases of HIV in the first six months of 2007, which is approximately the number of cases for all of 2006.[10] Health officials calculate that there were on average 200 new cases of HIV/AIDS infection in China each day in 2005.[11]

In 2007, China announced plans to spend 960 million yuan (US$127 million) on anti-retroviral drugs, expand public education, and conduct outreach to China's marginalized homosexual community.[12] The government also expanded policies to further incorporate foreign governments, international companies, grassroots organizations, and trade unions in its efforts to combat HIV/AIDS. In January 2007, the government, along with the International Labor Organization and the All-China Federation of Trade Unions, initiated a program that made HIV/AIDS education available in the workplace.[13] Privately owned Chinese firms are also gradually becoming involved in these efforts, often at the request of their foreign business affiliates.[14] In addition, the U.S. Department of Labor initiated a $3.5 million grant to support a program that focused on migrant workers.[15]

Nonetheless, while national officials have emphasized the importance of combating HIV/AIDS, it is local implementation that determines whether national-level commitment and policy action produce outcomes of consequence on the ground. Implementation remains highly problematic. Fear of the disease has led some local officials to harass persons with HIV/AIDS and their advocates.[16]

Henan province, where a large number of villagers contracted HIV through unsanitary blood collection practices in the late 1980s and early 1990s, provides a particularly stark example:

- In June 2003, public security officials, aided by local residents, raided Xiongqiao village, an "AIDS village" in Henan, and destroyed property, assaulted residents, and arrested 13 villagers. Villagers had appealed to local officials to receive previously promised government assistance for AIDS patients.[17]
- In May 2004, several people living with HIV/AIDS in Henan were detained for more than a week, apparently for seeking assistance from provincial officials to compel local officials to provide promised assistance.[18]
- In 2005, a U.S. NGO reported the violent closure of a privately run orphanage for children with AIDS in Henan, and another U.S. group noted that local officials in Henan have organized militias to prevent journalists and NGO observers from visiting AIDS patients.[19]
- In November 2005, public security officials detained activist Hu Jia, co-founder of two HIV/AIDS advocacy groups, when he attempted to deliver a petition on behalf of more than 50 AIDS patients to Vice Premier Wu Yi at a November 2005 AIDS conference in Henan. Citing government pressure, Hu subsequently resigned in February 2006 from one of the groups, Loving Source, and is currently under residential surveillance.[20]
- In November 2006, public officials detained HIV/AIDS advocacy group leader Wan Yanhai, forcing him to cancel a conference on AIDS, blood-transfusion safety, and legal human rights.[21]
- In February 2007, public security officials in Zhengzhou city, Henan, placed AIDS activist and doctor Gao Yaojie under surveillance at her home in an attempt to prevent her from traveling to the United States to accept a human rights award.[22] Central government officials intervened, and Gao was subsequently granted permission to travel to the United States to receive the 2007 Vital Voices Global Women's Leadership Award for Human Rights on March 14.[23]

The depth of the crisis is only magnified by official corruption. In July 2007, the Ministry of Health (MOH) announced the removal of a director of a Guangdong province blood center as a result of his involvement in illegal blood sales and noted that six other people had received sentences of between 6 and 18 months for helping individuals repeatedly sell their blood using fake identity cards.[24] In the hopes of reducing illegal blood trade activity, the MOH has announced that blood collection centers are required by the end of October 2007 to set up equipment to videotape plasma collections.[25]

A government advisor on AIDS policy has expressed concern that China's efforts to combat the disease have stalled and that funding, which in 2006 was 3 billion yuan (US$388 million), remains inadequate.[26] The government's commitment to provide care to specific subpopulations, such as children orphaned as a result of AIDS and ethnic minorities infected with HIV, appears to be wavering.[27] Sensitive issues, such as compensation for rural residents in central provinces who contracted HIV from the sale of blood, have hindered broader efforts to combat HIV/AIDS.[28]

At the local level, an overburdened, underfunded healthcare system makes it difficult for governments to provide the necessary prevention and treatment programs. Many programs lack sufficient numbers of qualified doctors to properly administer anti-retroviral drugs and to help patients maintain needed treatment, with the result that many patients simply drop out of the programs. Public education and awareness efforts have not fully succeeded: 66 percent of China's population reportedly continues to be unaware of how to protect themselves against HIV.[29] AIDS patients have also been discriminated against and denied treatment at hospitals.[30]

WIDESPREAD DISCRIMINATION AGAINST HEPATITIS B CARRIERS

China has a high rate of hepatitis B virus (HBV) infection, with 120 million carriers of the virus, who make up approximately 30 percent of the 400 million HBV carriers in the world.[31] Only 70 percent of China's population has been vaccinated for the disease. In an attempt to reduce hepatitis B infection, the Ministry of Health (MOH) issued the 2006–2010 National Plan on Hepatitis B Prevention and Control, with the top priority of strengthening vaccination programs, especially among young children. The goal is to lower the infection rate to 1 percent among those five years old and younger, and to less than 7 percent nationwide by 2010.[32]

Until 2004, there were no national laws protecting HBV carriers from discrimination in the workplace, and some central and local governments prohibited the hiring of people with certain varieties of the disease.[33] In April 2003, when university student Zhou Yichao was denied a public service job because he was an HBV carrier, he stabbed two officials in Zhejiang province, killing one. Zhou was later sentenced to death on murder charges.[34] This incident helped to spark discussion over the treatment of HBV carriers. In November 2003, HBV carrier Zhang Xianzhu of Anhui province successfully sued a government personnel office, complaining that his job application had been unjustly rejected. A court held in April 2004 that the personnel office applied the regulation incorrectly, but did not invalidate the regulation itself, and also denied Zhang's request to be reconsidered for the civil service position, noting that the recruitment season had already ended.[35] This was the first partially successful administrative lawsuit regarding discrimination against HBV carriers in the workplace.

In 2004, the National People's Congress (NPC) Standing Committee amended the Law on the Prevention and Control of Infectious Diseases to prohibit discrimination against persons with infectious diseases, persons carrying a pathogen of an infectious disease, and persons suspected of having an infectious disease.[36] In January 2005, the Ministry of Personnel and the MOH revised national standards to allow HBV carriers who do not exhibit symptoms of the disease to apply for employment with the government.[37]

Yet discrimination against HBV carriers remains widespread. Even though experts and Chinese officials have publicly stated that hepatitis B is not infectious in most work and school situations, many people believe that it is and refuse to hire HBV carriers or interact with them on those grounds.[38] A 2005 China Foundation for Hepatitis Prevention and Control survey, covering 583 hepatitis B patients in 18 provinces, found not only that a majority of Chinese physicians do not have adequate knowledge of hepatitis B or of ways to prevent and treat the disease, but also that 52 percent of the respondents had faced discrimination in employment and education.[39] In November 2005, two universities in the Xinjiang Uighur Autonomous Region (XUAR) suspended 156 students, diagnosed as hepatitis B positive in their matriculation medical examinations, from their studies for a year.[40] Students formed an action group and distributed fliers to protest this decision, and one student filed the first hepatitis B discrimination lawsuit in the XUAR against her university, Xinjiang Agricultural University.[41] The student eventually withdrew her case as university authorities allowed her to resume her studies amid widespread media coverage, and support from NGOs and concerned individuals.[42] As of December 2006, the other students were reportedly still not able to return to school.[43]

In September 2006, Urumqi municipal education officials in the XUAR expelled 19 high school students who had tested positive for hepatitis B.[44] After first attempting to petition local government bureaus, seven families later filed a lawsuit against the municipal education bureau, with the hope that the students would be allowed to continue their education.[45] The Urumqi Tianshan District People's Court postponed the hearing date on several occasions until it announced on November 20 that the families had withdrawn their case. The families' lawyer and a NGO that works on hepatitis B issues believe that the case was dropped due to pressure from local officials and employers.[46] In addition, public security officials forced Snow Lotus, an unregistered NGO based in the XUAR, to close in October and discontinue its work for reportedly drafting open letters on behalf of the students and breaking the story to the media.[47] [See Section III—Civil Society for more information on this case.] Local education officials maintain that the students were expelled in order to protect other pupils, yet central officials and experts have condemned the expulsion.[48] According to Mao Qun'an, a MOH representative, "This is prejudice. All these students can go to school unless they are sick enough to be hospitalized."[49]

Most recently, a 2007 survey on health discrimination in the workplace found that 49 percent of respondents would be unwilling to work with HBV carriers, and 55 percent noted that they would not hire HBV carriers.[50] Employer screening for HBV remains common, especially in cities.[51] A Chinese job applicant filed a lawsuit against Nokia in March 2007, alleging that its China branch denied him employment after he underwent a company medical examination and was found to be a HBV carrier.[52] The applicant is claiming 500,000 yuan (US$66,613) in emotional damages in what is reportedly the first hepatitis B discrimination case against a foreign multinational company in China.[53] The Dongguan People's Court accepted the case in May, and court proceedings began on August 15 and concluded with a decision by the judge to select a retrial date.[54] At press time, the court has yet to publicly issue a decision or a retrial date. In some online forums, there is active discussion of this case, as well as other cases of discrimination against HBV carriers.[55]

In May 2007, the MOH and the Ministry of Labor and Social Security issued a non-legally binding opinion to protect the employment rights of HBV carriers, including a prohibition against mandatory HBV screening for job applicants, except for those positions that were previously designated as forbidden for HBV carriers.[56] On August 30, 2007, the NPC Standing Committee adopted the Employment Promotion Law, which stipulates provisions that could benefit HBV carriers seeking employment.[57] For example, Article 30 of the new law prohibits employers from refusing to hire applicants on the grounds that they carry infectious diseases, except for those industries barred to formally certified infectious disease carriers because of the possibility that they might spread the disease, and Article 62 allows workers to file a lawsuit against employers who violate provisions of the new law and discriminate against employees.[58] Without the concurrent creation of effective programs to raise public awareness of how the disease is spread, incentives for local implementation, and a clear and comprehensive definition of discrimination,[59] the impact of these regulatory measures remains to be seen.[60]

STATE CONTROL OF INFORMATION RELATING TO SARS AND AVIAN FLU

In July 2007, military officials denied Dr. Jiang Yanyong permission to travel to the United States to receive a human rights award. Dr. Jiang had previously informed foreign media of government attempts to cover up the SARS outbreak in 2003.[61] In addition, Chinese laws still require journalists to get advance approval before publishing public health information about broad categories of diseases classified as "state secrets."

Chinese public health officials sought to improve their ability to prevent and control the spread of avian flu by improving the flow of information between lower officials and higher officials following the mishandling of the SARS epidemic in 2003. The State Council issued regulations in November 2005 requiring provincial governments to report "major" animal epidemics to the State Council within four hours of discovering them, and county and city governments to report cases to provincial authorities within two hours. Officials who are found negligent in reporting outbreaks face removal from office and potential prosecution.[62]

Such laws allow for improved internal channels of information but do not necessarily guarantee free flow of information to the public. The Law on the Protection of State Secrets and implementing regulations in the area of public health continue to serve as a hindrance to the free flow of information on public health matters. For example, the Regulation on State Secrets and the Specific Scope of Each Level of Secrets in Public Health Work, issued in 1996, categorize as state secrets information on large-scale epidemics of viral hepatitis and other diseases that has not been authorized for public disclosure by the government.[63] A new national Regulation on the Public Disclosure of Government Information, issued in April 2007, contains provisions that require agencies to disclose information on public health supervision and sudden emergencies, but these "state secret" exceptions remain in place.[64] [See Section II—Freedom of Expression.]

HEALTHCARE SYSTEM REFORM

During the 1980s, the government abolished its previous rural healthcare system, which was based on village clinics staffed by "barefoot doctors" and financed by cooperative insurance.[65] The government did not replace the previous system with a new rural cooperative medical system until 2003.[66] From 1977 to 2002, the number of doctors in rural China decreased from 1.8 million to 800,000, and the number of rural healthcare workers decreased from 3.4 million to 800,000.[67] Eighty percent of medical resources are now concentrated in cities.[68] The rural-urban disparity is also apparent in mortality statistics. Residents of large cities in China live 12 years longer than rural residents, and the infant mortality rate in some rural areas is nine times higher than in large cities.[69]

Urban Healthcare

The government established a public health insurance program for employed urban residents in 1998, and by the end of 2006, approximately 160 million out of the country's 500 million urban residents received coverage.[70] In July 2007, Premier Wen Jiabao announced plans to establish a national health insurance program to cover all urban residents, including children, the elderly, and the uninsured, over the next three years. The central government has selected 79 cities to launch pilot programs by the end of September 2007.[71] In order to improve community-level medical services in urban areas, large city hospitals will provide facility and staff support to community health clinics, and a data-sharing system will be established.[72]

Rural Healthcare

Under China's Rural Cooperative Medical System (RCMS), a farmer and each family member that participates in the system pays an average premium of 10 yuan (US$1.25) each year into a personal medical care account, with governments at all levels subsidizing an additional 40 yuan (US$5) on average.[73] Participants may have up to 65 percent of their healthcare costs reimbursed, but are required to first pay such costs out of pocket.[74] The scope of the RCMS's coverage, and government spending on healthcare, has increased in recent years. The government reported that the number of counties covered by the RCMS increased from 687 pilot counties in 2005 to 1,451 counties (50.7 percent of China's rural areas) at the end of 2006.[75] Prior to implementation of the RCMS, the percentage of rural residents with health insurance coverage reportedly reached a low of 7 percent in 2002.[76] After the RCMS was introduced in 2003, the government reported that coverage had increased to 51 percent by February 2007.[77] The amount of money the central government has announced it plans to spend on rural healthcare also increased from 2.073 billion yuan (US$252 million) in 2004 to 5.8 billion yuan (US$750 million) in 2006, and reportedly to 10.1 billion yuan (US$1.33 billion) in 2007.[78] Since the establishment of the RCMS, some areas have reported increases in the number of hospitalized patients and in the amount of revenue for local clinics.[79]

Rising Cost of Healthcare

Some senior Chinese officials and scholars have questioned the fairness and efficiency of the medical and healthcare system. The poorest residents in rural areas frequently do not enroll in the cooperatives because they cannot afford the required fee. As many as 50 percent of farmers who fall ill do not seek healthcare for economic reasons, and half of all children who die in rural areas had not received medical treatment.[80] For rural participants especially, the reimbursement level remains inadequate. The average reimbursement rate is 27.5 percent, determined in part by the specific disease and the local government's budget.[81] Many counties and townships do not have the financial resources to supply their portion of the fund. In addition, rural clinics are poorly funded and lack adequate medical personnel and equipment.[82]

High medical costs have become the top concern of Chinese citizens, according to a 2006 Chinese Academy of Social Sciences survey on "Problems that Affect Social Harmony and Stability," with medical expenses comprising 11.8 percent of an average family's total annual spending.[83] There has also been an increase in violent attacks on doctors and hospital personnel as citizens protest rising costs, medical errors, and declining professional ethics.[84] In 2006, hospitals reported 9,831 cases of violence, more than 200 million yuan (US$25.6 million) in damages to hospital facilities, and 5,519 medical personnel injuries, an increase from 5,093 cases of violence, 67 million yuan (US$8.8 million) in damages, and 2,600 medical personnel injuries in 2002.[85]

To address some of these issues, the Ministry of Health relocated approximately 5,500 doctors and nurses from urban areas to rural areas in 2007 to treat rural patients and train local medical personnel.[86] In addition, the central government has set a goal of renovating 22,000 village clinics, 1,300 county-level general hospitals, 400 county-level traditional or ethnic minority hospitals, and 950 county-level maternity and childcare institutes by 2010, and has pledged more than 20 billion yuan (US$2.5 billion) for the task.[87]

HUMAN TRAFFICKING

INTRODUCTION

The Chinese government has taken some steps to establish a national-level anti-trafficking coordinating mechanism, to increase public awareness, to expand the availability of some social services for victims of trafficking, and to improve international cooperation. The Chinese government reports that efforts have led to a decline in some forms of trafficking, but also notes that there has been an increase in other forms of trafficking that have not received as much attention, such as using trafficking victims to perform forced labor or engage in commercial sex. Within the past five years, for example, there has been a rise in cross-border trafficking cases, with internal and international traffickers increasingly working together. The U.S. State Department also notes that the Chinese government "continued to treat North Korean victims of trafficking as economic migrants, routinely deporting them back to horrendous conditions in North Korea." [1]

The National People's Congress Standing Committee revised the PRC Law on the Protection of Minors on December 29, 2006, which became effective June 1, 2007, to explicitly prohibit the trafficking of minors.[2] Article 41 of the revised law contains new provisions that prohibit the trafficking, kidnapping, and maltreatment, including sexual exploitation, of minors, although these terms are not defined.[3] In July 2007, the All-China Women's Federation (ACWF) and the Ministry of Public Security (MPS) held the first National Anti-Trafficking Children's Forum, in which an MPS spokesperson noted the increase in the number of cases of forced labor trafficking and trafficking for commercial sexual exploitation, and an annual decrease in the number of cases handled by the MPS that relate to the trafficking of women and children for marriage and adoption.[4]

Official Chinese case statistics suggest, however, that China is either not publishing accurate data on the incidence of human trafficking, uses non-standard categories for these crimes, or has low prosecution rates in these cases. In 2005, the MPS reported that Chinese police departments nationwide opened 2,884 cases of "abducting women and children," of which they reported "investigating and handling" just over 2,400 cases. In 2006, the total number of cases investigated and resolved was just over 2,100. Police press reports portray the trends as evidence that such abduction cases have declined in society since the 1980s and 1990s, and as proof of the "obvious effectiveness" of their policies.[5] By contrast, the U.S. State Department's 2007 Trafficking in Persons Report notes that "an estimated minimum of 10,000 to 20,000 victims" are trafficked internally each year.[6] The ACWF–MPS forum also touched on legal protections for trafficking victims. According to the MPS spokesperson, "In trafficking and abduction aspects, China's legal protection is underdeveloped, and it needs to be further strengthened."[7] The forum noted, for example, that China's Criminal Law provides punishment for the trafficking of women and children, but neglects minors over 14 and male adults, who are often targeted for forced labor.[8]

China's Ministry of Public Security reports that efforts to combat human trafficking have led to a decline in some forms of trafficking, but that there has also been an increase in other forms of trafficking that have not received as much attention, such as using trafficking victims to perform forced labor.[9] As the U.S. State Department reports in its annual review of global human trafficking, China "is a source, transit, and destination country" for human trafficking.[10] Domestic trafficking continues to comprise the majority of trafficking cases in China. Women and children, who make up 90 percent of the cases, are trafficked from poorer provinces to more prosperous provinces on the east coast.[11] Some experts note that the Chinese government's attention to human trafficking for commercial sexual exploitation appears to be uneven, with far greater concern shown towards the internal trafficking of Chinese girls and women and little concern over foreign girls and women who are trafficked into China or who enter China voluntarily but are subsequently trafficked. Many of these women are from Vietnam, North Korea, and Mongolia, among other countries, and are treated as immigration violators who are detained and subsequently repatriated.[12]

There have also been increases in the number of cross-border trafficking cases and, especially between 2004 and 2006, an increase in the number of infant trafficking cases.[13] The rising number of infant trafficking cases in China reflects many factors, such as China's population planning policies, economic disparity, and a lack of awareness among the general public [see Section II—Population Planning]. Most of the infants who have been rescued were male, but the increased demand for children has reportedly driven traffickers to traffic females as well.[14] Some of the cases involved social service organizations buying infants that had been abducted, and selling them to adoptive families at marked-up prices, as well as traffickers buying infants from private medical clinics and other social service organizations and selling them to buyers elsewhere.[15] In 2007, the U.S. State Department placed China on its Tier Two Watch List for the third consecutive year due to the Chinese government's failure to show evidence of efforts to improve comprehensive victim protection services and to address trafficking of persons for forced labor.[16]

INTERNATIONAL LAWS AND OBLIGATIONS

The Chinese government ratified the UN Convention against Transnational Organized Crime on September 23, 2003, but still has not ratified its protocol that addresses trafficking in persons. The protocol represents the first global legally binding definition of trafficking in persons and aims to support international cooperation in investigating and prosecuting cases and in protecting and assisting victims of trafficking.[17] In addition, China has ratified the Convention to Eliminate All Forms of Discrimination against Women and the Convention on the Rights of the Child, which further legally bind the Chinese government to suppress and prevent the abduction and trafficking of women and children.[18]

DOMESTIC EFFORTS TO COMBAT HUMAN TRAFFICKING AND CHALLENGES

Central and local governments have taken steps to combat trafficking within the past five years, but these initiatives remain inadequate to effectively address the root causes of human trafficking and forms of trafficking such as forced labor. For example, Article 39 of the Law on the Protection of Women's Rights and Interests (LPWRI), which was amended in 2005, expanded the number of organizations responsible for preventing trafficking in women and rehabilitating victims, including local women's federations and local public security, labor, social security, and health bureaus.[19] The central government announced in 2007 that it will establish a national-level anti-trafficking coordinating mechanism that aims to strengthen interagency cooperation, as at least seven agencies currently have regulatory responsibilities to combat trafficking.[20]

The 2003 and 2004 Commission Annual Reports noted that the central government initiated several short-term "Strike Hard" campaigns to punish traffickers and rescue victims.[21] But these campaigns have not proven to be effective instruments that address the causes of trafficking, nor do they introduce administrative and legal mechanisms to combat future trafficking operations. "Strike Hard" campaigns have also been characterized by extensive violations of criminal procedure rights.[22] Some provincial and municipal governments have localized efforts to combat trafficking by creating short-term rehabilitation centers, and increasing public awareness efforts that inform people of their legal protections and resource options.[23] For example, Sichuan provincial public security officials have created informational fliers, public service announcements, and pamphlets that explain legal protections, resources, and hotline numbers that are aimed at migrant workers and other workers who are most at risk.[24] In addition, within the past year, Yunnan provincial authorities held a media outreach seminar to raise awareness among journalists of anti-trafficking strategies, victim protection, and relevant legislation.[25]

These preliminary steps are positive, but local governments need to expand them to include more comprehensive victim rehabilitation services such as psychological counseling and long-term care. While there are currently legal prohibitions against some types of human trafficking, these protections do not prohibit forms of trafficking such as debt bondage or commercial sexual exploitation that involves coercion or fraud.[26] Another hurdle is the difficulty central government officials face in compelling local law enforcement officials to aggressively pursue cases that cross jurisdictional boundaries, especially as more trafficking cases take place across provincial and national borders.[27] For example, U.S. experts have noted that "local Party dominance over law enforcement creates powerful incentives for local police departments to neglect their responsibilities to share crime-related data and intelligence with other jurisdictions."[28]

INTERNATIONAL COOPERATION

Central and local governments have increased cooperation with other countries to investigate and prosecute trafficking cases involving women and children. In particular, the Chinese government has discussed trafficking in persons with the United States as part of the bilateral China-U.S. Global Issues Forum, and has worked to improve its cross-border prosecution efforts with such countries as Vietnam.[29] China is also actively cooperating with international organizations such as the International Labor Organization, the International Organization for Migration, and the United Nations Interagency Project on Human Trafficking in the Greater Mekong Sub-region on programs to prevent and combat human trafficking.[30] The Chinese government has prepared a National Plan of Action to address the trafficking of women and children, which it still has not adopted.[31] A September 4, 2007, China Daily article noted that the government hopes to adopt the national action plan by the end of 2007.[32]

North Korean Refugees in China

In 2006–2007, China continued to fail in its obligations to the thousands of North Korean refugees who crossed its northeastern border to escape North Korea's chronic food shortages and political oppression. While an accurate estimate of the size of this underground population is probably not possible, in recent years the U.S. State Department and several NGOs have estimated that 20,000 to 50,000 North Koreans currently are hiding in northeastern China. Chinese civilian, law enforcement and military experts speaking in 2005–2006 typically cited an estimate of 30,000 to 50,000.[1] An October 2006 report by the International Crisis Group surveyed the opinions of many NGO experts and reached an estimate that the total number of North Korean refugees residing on Chinese soil is approximately 100,000.[2] As noted by the State Department's 2007 Trafficking in Persons (TIP) report, these refugees, many of whom are women, are unable to work legally in China. Thus, many of them are highly vulnerable to being kidnapped by traffickers:

> The illegal status of North Koreans in the People's Republic of China (P.R.C.) and other Southeast Asian countries increases their vulnerability to trafficking schemes and sexual and physical abuse. In the most common form of trafficking, North Korean women and children who voluntarily cross the border into P.R.C. are picked up by trafficking rings and sold as brides to P.R.C. nationals, usually of Korean ethnicity, or placed in forced labor. In a less common form of trafficking, North Korean women and girls are lured out of North Korea by the promise of food, jobs, and freedom, only to be forced into prostitution, marriage, or exploitative labor arrangements once in P.R.C.[3]

The U.S. State Department reports that during 2006 "several thousand North Koreans were reportedly detained and forcibly returned to North Korea."[4] To encourage these repatriation efforts, central government authorities assign local public security bureaus in northeastern China a target number of North Koreans that they must detain in order to receive favorable work evaluations.[5] To persuade civilians in these areas not to assist the refugees, the government also provides financial rewards to citizens who reveal the locations of refugees.[6] By employing these incentive and punishment systems on citizens to turn these refugees in, China deliberately undermines its own international legal obligations to refrain from repatriating North Koreans and further deters its citizens from supplying humanitarian assistance. In the past several years, the government has reportedly built new detention centers along the Chinese-Mongolian border and the Chinese-North Korean border in order to accommodate more North Koreans before it repatriates them.[7]

By returning these refugees to the DPRK , China is in contravention of its obligations under the 1951 Convention relating to the Status of Refugees (1951 Convention) and its 1967 Protocol (Protocol). Under the 1951 Convention and its Protocol, no contracting state may "expel or return ('refouler') a refugee in any manner whatsoever to the frontiers of territories where his life or freedom would be threatened on account of his race, religion, nationality, membership of a particular social group or political opinion." [8]

The Chinese government classifies all North Koreans who enter China without documents as illegal economic migrants without making any effort to determine whether or not they are refugees, and claims that it must return them to the DPRK. In a June 19, 2007, press conference Ministry of Foreign Affairs press spokesperson Qin Gang repeated China's longstanding insistence that these migrants "came to China for economic reasons and they are not 'refugees' at all." [9] In addition, the Chinese government bases its policy of repatriating North Koreans on a 1961 treaty with the DPRK and a series of protocols on border management signed by the two countries in 1986 and 1998. [10] But China is also obligated under Article 3 of the Convention Against Torture not to forcibly return any person to another state where there are substantial grounds for believing that he or she would be in danger of torture. [11] Under the general international legal principle of non-derogation, China's bilateral commitments with the DPRK should not supersede China's international obligations under the 1951 Convention, its Protocol, and the Convention Against Torture. [12]

Moreover, the treatment these refugees receive upon their repatriation to the DPRK provides more than ample evidence that they satisfy the definition of refugees under international law. The 1951 Convention defines a refugee as someone who, "owing to well-founded fear of being persecuted for reasons of race, religion, nationality, membership of a particular social group or political opinion, is outside the country of his nationality and is unable or, owing to such fear, is unwilling to avail himself of the protection of that country." [13] In a 2005 report, the UN Special Rapporteur on Human Rights in North Korea noted that even North Koreans who have crossed into China for reasons of livelihood are nevertheless "refugees sur place," a designation for those who "did not leave their country of origin for fear of persecution, but who fear persecution upon return." [14]

The DPRK government imprisons, tortures, and executes repatriated North Koreans, and has increased the punishment for border crossers since late 2004. Article 233 of the amended North Korean Penal Code provides for up to two years' imprisonment for citizens who leave the DPRK without permission, and Article 62 provides for no less than five years' imprisonment for defectors, and life imprisonment or execution for defectors deemed to have committed "an extremely grave offense." [15] According to international NGOs, North Koreans are considered to have committed a more serious offense, and are punished more harshly, if they have converted to Christianity or have met with Christian missionaries, South Koreans, or other foreigners while in China. [16] In late 2004, the North Korean government changed its policy toward repatriated border crossers to increase prison sentences from several months to several years and to detain them in regular prisons, which have harsher regimes, rather than labor camps. [17] Defector testimonies document cases of beatings, forced labor, lack of food and medicine, degrading treatment, torture, and execution. [18] Pregnant female defectors have reportedly been subjected to forced abortions under poor medical care. According to a South Korean Bar Association study, defectors have also reported witnessing North Korean authorities carry out forced abortions.[19]

The Chinese government blanketly asserts that North Korean migrants are not refugees, and does not permit individual petitions for asylum. The government also denies the UN High Commissioner for Refugees (UNHCR) and other organizations the access needed to evaluate their claims. Chinese guards posted outside the UNHCR office and foreign embassies in Beijing block access to North Koreans who seek to present refugee petitions.[20] The government's failure to allow for a process in order to evaluate whether individual North Koreans have reason to fear persecution upon return to the DPRK contravenes its obligations under the 1951 Convention and its Protocol, as identified by the U.S. Committee for Human Rights in North Korea: "Implicit in the Convention—the strict Article 33 prohibition read together with the multi-pronged Article 1 refugee definition—is a requirement that states take appropriate steps to determine whether an individual is a refugee before sending him or her back to possible persecution."[21] This refusal of access by the UNHCR also contravenes Article 35 of the 1951 Convention.[22]

The government fines and imprisons Chinese citizens and international humanitarian workers who assist North Korean refugees, and these penalties have recently been increased. In 2006, Chinese authorities sentenced Hong Jin-hee, Kim Hong-kyun, and Lee Soo-cheol, three South Korean citizens and former North Korean defectors, to seven, five, and two years' imprisonment, respectively, for assisting North Koreans in China to seek asylum in a third country. Chinese authorities detained Kim and Lee in Beijing in October 2004, and Hong in Shenyang in November 2004, and have held the three without trial until their sentencing in 2006.[23] In November 2006, authorities in Yantai city, Shandong province, released on parole Choi Yong-hoon, a South Korean citizen imprisoned for assisting North Koreans in China to seek asylum in South Korea, after Choi served 3 years and 11 months of his 5-year sentence.[24]

The Chinese government is reportedly in the final stages of drafting a Regulation on the Administration of Refugees.[25] A June 2007 report in the official People's Daily said that "the government draft national refugee regulation [is] now in its final phase," but that "[i]t is unclear when the draft will be submitted to the State Council for final review and approval." The report also mentions the UNHCR role in "helping . . . [to] draft" the regulation.[26] In March 2006, the UNHCR said that his office would be involved in insuring that the regulation is in compliance with international law.[27] The drafting process for these regulations provides Chinese officials with an opportunity to carry out a long overdue reassessment of their refugee policies to make them accessible and transparent, providing every refugee with a chance for a legal hearing and an appeal if necessary.

Freedom of Residence and Travel

FREEDOM OF RESIDENCE

The Chinese government continues to enforce the household registration (*hukou*) system it first established in the 1950s. This system limits the right of Chinese citizens to determine their permanent place of residence. Regulations and policies that condition legal rights and access to social services on residency status have resulted in discrimination against rural *hukou* holders who migrate for work to urban areas. The *hukou* system exacerbates barriers that migrant workers and their families face in areas such as employment, healthcare, property rights, legal compensation, and schooling. [See Section II—Worker Rights for more information.] Central and local government reforms from the past five years have mitigated some obstacles to equal treatment, but provisions that allow people to change *hukou* status have included criteria that advantage those with greater economic and educational resources or with family connections to urban *hukou* holders.[1] The government's restrictions on residence and discrimination in equal treatment contravene international human rights standards,[2] including those in treaties China has signed or ratified.[3] In May 2005, the UN Committee on Economic, Social, and Cultural Rights expressed "deep concern" over the discrimination resulting from "inter alia, the restrictive national household registration system (*hukou*) which continues to be in place despite official announcements regarding reforms."[4]

Recent reforms have addressed some of the burdens migrants face. In 2001, the State Council expanded an earlier program to allow rural migrants who meet set requirements to migrate to small towns and cities and obtain *hukou* there, while keeping rural land rights.[5] In 2003, the State Council abolished "Measures for the Custody and Repatriation of Vagrant Beggars in Cities" that allowed the police to detain, at will, people without identification, residence, or work permits.[6] The same year, the State Council issued a national legal aid regulation that does not condition legal aid on residence status.[7]

Central government directives promulgated in 2003 and beyond also have called for reform, though many have had limited formal legal force and limited impact.

- In 2003, the State Council issued a directive acknowledging migrants' right to work in cities, forbidding discriminatory policies, and calling for improved services for migrants and their families.[8]
- Also in 2003, the State Council issued legal guidance ordering urban governments to take responsibility for educating migrant children.[9]
- A 2004 State Council directive called for an end to discriminatory work restrictions against migrants.[10]
- The Ministry of Labor and Social Services (MOLSS) issued a labor handbook the following year stating that the MOLSS will not require migrants to obtain a work registration card in their place of origin before seeking jobs in urban areas.[11]

- A joint opinion on the promotion of a "new socialist countryside" issued in 2005 by the Communist Party Central Committee and the State Council called for reforms to the *hukou* system, including a reiteration of prior reform measures that stalled at the local level.[12]
- In 2006, the State Council issued an opinion addressing various issues affecting migrant workers and calling for measures to ease, under certain conditions, migrants' ability to settle in urban areas.[13]
- 2006 revisions to the compulsory education law codify a guarantee of equal educational opportunities for children outside the jurisdiction of their *hukou* registry.[14]
- During the 10th session of the National People's Congress (NPC) in March 2007, Chinese legislators approved a resolution creating a delegate quota in the NPC reserved for migrant workers.[15]
- In 2007, the Ministry of Public Security formulated a series of proposals to submit to the State Council for approval.[16] Major reforms in the proposal include improving the temporary residence permit system, improving the ability of migrants' spouses and parents to transfer *hukou* to urban areas, and using the existence of a fixed and legal place of residence as the primary basis for obtaining registration in a city of residence.[17]

Uneven implementation of *hukou* reform at the local level has dulled the impact of national calls for change. Fiscal burdens placed on local governments have served as disincentives for implementing reforms. Fears of population pressures and citizen activism, in addition to discriminatory attitudes against migrants, also have fueled resistance from local governments.[18] Since 2001, many provinces and large cities have implemented measures that allow migrants to obtain an urban *hukou*, but they generally give preference to wealthier and more educated migrants by conditioning change in status on meeting requirements such as having "a stable place of residence" and a "stable source of income," as defined in local provisions.[19] New reforms instituted in Chengdu in 2006 allow some migrants to obtain a *hukou* where they rent housing in the city and reside in it for over a year, but the reforms also impose conditions that disadvantage poorer migrants.[20] Other policies also are detrimental to broader reforms of the *hukou* system. In 2005, authorities in Shenzhen implemented tighter restrictions against migrants by suspending the processing of *hukou* applications for migrants' dependents. Authorities also said they would limit the growth of private schools for migrant children and require migrant parents to pay additional fees to enroll their children in public schools.[21] In 2006, Shenyang municipal authorities reversed 2003 relaxations on *hukou* requirements when they reinstituted temporary residence requirements for migrants.[22]

Some local government measures have been beneficial to improving conditions for migrants. After the State Council called in 2004 for abolishing employment restrictions for migrants, the Beijing municipal government followed suit with local reforms in 2005 that eliminated restrictions on migrant workers holding certain occupations.[23] In 2005, Henan provincial authorities reported that they would institute measures to increase migrant workers' access to healthcare while in urban areas.[24] In 2006, authorities in a district within the city of Xi'an reported instituting measures granting all residents equal access to social services.[25] Some local governments have removed discriminatory compensation levels for rural migrants. In October 2006, the Chongqing High People's Court issued an opinion stipulating that rural migrants who have resided in Chongqing for over a year and have an "appropriate source of income" are entitled to the same compensation as urban *hukou* holders in traffic accident cases.[26] The Supreme People's Court is currently contemplating a new judicial interpretation on the role of *hukou* status in determining death compensation rates.[27]

Central and local governments have accompanied measures to address discrimination against migrants with calls to strengthen supervision over migrant populations, reflecting concerns over perceived social unrest. The 2003 directive articulating broad protections for migrant workers also supports measures to increase control over them, including through "social order management responsibility systems."[28] Although a government official called in 2005 for transforming management techniques from methods of control to methods of service,[29] authorities have continued to enact measures to exert government control. A circular from Henan province issued in 2006 called for monitoring migrants by keeping files on their rental housing.[30]

FREEDOM OF TRAVEL

The Chinese government continues to enforce restrictions on citizens' right to travel, in violation of international human rights standards.[31] The Law on Passports, effective January 2007, articulates some beneficial features for passport applicants, but gives officials the discretion to refuse a passport where "[t]he competent organs of the State Council believe that [the applicant's] leaving China will do harm to the state security or result in serious losses to the benefits of the state."[32] Authorities restrict travel to penalize citizens who express views they deem objectionable. The Chinese government initially failed to approve democracy activist Yang Jianli's passport application,[33] which he submitted after his release from prison in April 2007.[34] In August, however, authorities allowed Yang to travel to the United States. Authorities had detained Yang in 2002 when he crossed into China on another person's passport. Authorities had earlier refused to renew his passport and had barred him and other activists from entering the country.[35] Chinese officials have prevented other activists from traveling abroad, including rights defender Tang Jingling, whose passport was confiscated by Guangdong border authorities in September 2006 as he was en route to New York. Tang brought an administrative lawsuit against the government in December 2006.[36] In February 2007, the government prevented a group of writers from participating in a conference in Hong Kong by denying visas to some writers, warning others not to attend, and directly preventing some from passing through border controls into Hong Kong.[37] [See Section II—Freedom of Expression for more information.] In June 2007, authorities intercepted human rights defenders Yao Lifa and Zeng Jinyan at the airport and prevented them from traveling to an overseas human rights conference.[38] In July, authorities rejected Mongol rights advocate Gao Yulian's passport application on the grounds of "possible harm to state security and national interests."[39] In August, Shanghai authorities denied the passport applications of rights defense lawyer and former political prisoner Zheng Enchong and his spouse Jiang Meili.[40] The same month, authorities in Beijing prevented Yuan Weijing, spouse of imprisoned rights activist Chen Guangcheng, from traveling overseas to accept an award for her husband.[41] In 2007, authorities also denied passport applications from the family members of defense lawyer Gao Zhisheng.[42]

The government also uses travel restrictions to control religious citizens' overseas travel and to punish religious adherents deemed to act outside approved parameters. [See Section II—Freedom of Religion for more information.] The central government has increased control over Muslims' ability to undertake overseas religious pilgrimages, especially since 2004. In June 2007, overseas media reported that authorities in the Xinjiang Uighur Autonomous Region (XUAR) implemented a policy to confiscate passports from Muslims, and Uighurs in particular, in a reported effort to enforce restrictions on overseas pilgrimages.[43] In July, the XUAR government announced the public security bureau would strengthen passport controls as part of its campaign to curb unauthorized pilgrimages.[44] House church leader Zhang Rongliang, who resorted to obtaining illegal travel documents after the government refused to issue him a passport, was sentenced to seven and one-half years' imprisonment in 2006 on charges of illegally crossing the border and fraudulently obtaining a passport.[45] Also in 2006, authorities detained two leaders of the unregistered Wenzhou diocese, Peter Shao Zhumin and Paul Jiang Surang, after they returned from a pilgrimage to Rome. Six months after their detention, Shao and Jiang received prison sentences of 9 and 11 months, respectively, after authorities accused them of falsifying their passports and charged them with illegal exit from the country.[46] Authorities placed house church historian and former political prisoner Zhang Yinan and his family under surveillance in 2006 after he tried to apply for a passport to attend a religious function in the United States.[47]

Endnotes

Notes to Section II—Status of Women
¹ CECC, 2003 Annual Report, 2 October 03, 47.
² Ibid., 47–49; CECC, 2004 Annual Report, 5 October 04, 56–57; CECC, 2006 Annual Report, 20 September 06, 97–98.
³ CECC, 2004 Annual Report, 55–56; CECC, 2005 Annual Report, 11 October 05, 67, 69; CECC, 2006 Annual Report, 99.
⁴ CECC, 2004 Annual Report, 56–58; CECC, 2005 Annual Report, 67–68; CECC, 2006 Annual Report, 97–99.
⁵ CECC, 2005 Annual Report, 67; CECC, 2006 Annual Report, 97–98.
⁶ PRC Constitution, art. 48. Article 48 declares that women are equal to men and names women as a "vulnerable social group" requiring special protection.
⁷ The State Council Women's Development Program, 2001–2010 [Zhongguo funü fazhan gangyao, 2001–2010], May 2001.
⁸ PRC Law on the Protection of Women's Rights and Interests, enacted 3 April 92, amended 28 August 05; CECC, 2005 Annual Report, 67–68.
⁹ These include Liaoning province (2006), Heilongjiang province (2006), Jiangxi province (2006), Hunan province (2006), Shaanxi province (2006), Xinjiang province (2006), Wenzhou municipality (2006), Shanghai municipality (2007), and Guangdong province (2007), among others. See "Wenzhou City Issues New Domestic Violence Provisions," CECC China Human Rights and Rule of Law Update, December 2006, 16–17; "Regarding the Amended Shanghai Law on the Protection of Women's Rights and Interests Implementing Measures," People's Daily (Online), 11 May 07; Xulin and Sun Xiaosu, "Married-out Women in Guangdong Province Gain Hope," China Women's News, reprinted in Women Watch—China (Online), 7 June 07.
¹⁰ "Regarding the Amended Shanghai Law on the Protection of Women's Rights and Interests Implementing Measures," People's Daily.
¹¹ CECC, 2002–2004 Annual Reports.
¹² CECC Staff Interview; "Wenzhou City Issues New Domestic Violence Provisions," CECC China Human Rights and Rule of Law Update, 16–17; "System of Laws and Policies Protecting Women Take a Step Closer Toward Completion" [Fu bao falü zhengce tixi jinyibu wanshan], Legal Daily (Online), 29 January 07; "Regarding the Amended Shanghai Law on the Protection of Women's Rights and Interests Implementing Measures," People's Daily; Wang Zhuqiong, "New Move To Stem Domestic Violence," China Daily (Online), 21 July 07.
¹³ Committee on the Elimination of Discrimination Against Women, Concluding Comments of the Committee on the Elimination of Discrimination Against Women, Advanced Unedited Version, Thirty-sixth session, 7–25 August 06.
¹⁴ PRC Marriage Law, enacted 10 September 80, amended 28 April 01, art 3; PRC Law on the Protection of Women's Rights and Interests, art. 46; "Same Domestic Violence Accusation, Different Results in Shanghai and Baotou Court Cases; Expert Calls for Unified Standard" [Tongshi shou nuesha fu Shanghai Baotou pan butong zhuanjia: tongyi biaozhun], Legal Daily (Online), 30 March 06; Human Rights in China (Online), "Implementation of the Convention of the Elimination of All Forms of Discrimination Against Women in the People's Republic of China, A Parallel NGO Report," June 2006.
¹⁵ For example, with regards to domestic violence survivors bearing the burden in bringing complaints, see the PRC Marriage Law, arts. 43, 45.
¹⁶ "Domestic Violence in Spotlight," China Daily (Online), 2 August 07; "Survey of Young Female Migrant Workers Reveals 70 Percent Have Been Sexually Harassed" [Hunan nianqing nüxing nongmingong diaocha 7 cheng dagongmei zaoguo xingsaorao], Xinhua (Online), 15 May 06.
¹⁷ CECC, 2003 Annual Report, 47–48.
¹⁸ Ibid., 48.
¹⁹ Committee on the Elimination of Discrimination Against Women, Concluding Comments of the Committee on the Elimination of Discrimination Against Women, 4.
²⁰ CECC, 2006 Annual Report, 99.
²¹ CECC, 2004 Annual Report, 56.
²² "Women Contribute to over 40% GDP," China News, reprinted in All-China Women's Federation (Online), 17 May 07.
²³ Guo Aibing, "More Women Fill Top Posts, but Still Wield Little Authority," South China Morning Post (Online), 16 May 07; "Women Contribute to over 40% GDP," China News; "Minimum Hiring Rate for Women Employees Must Be 30%" [Luyong gongwuyuan nüxingbili bude diyu 30%], China Women's News (Online), 15 January 07.
²⁴ "Chengdu Imposes Gender Quota on Local Government's Leading Positions" [Chengdu guiding quxian si da banxi zhishao ge you yi ming nü ganbu], Eastday Net (Online), 7 November 06; Standing Committee of Heilongjiang People's Congress, "Law Guaranteeing Gender Ratio of Heilongjiang People's Congress, Implementing Women's Law, Appears" [Renda nü daibiao bili tigao dao 30% funü quanyi baozhang fa shishi banfa chutai], 31 October 06; "Funds for Women's Development Work are No Lower than 0.3 yuan Per Person" [Funü gongzuo jingfei meiren mei nian bu diyu 0.3 yuan], China Women's News (Online), 31 October 06.
²⁵ CECC, 2005 Annual Report, 69–70.
²⁶ Specifically, women accounted for 27.8 percent of all reported HIV/AIDS cases in 2006, an increase from 19.4 percent in 2000. "More than a Quarter of AIDS Patients in China are Women," Xinhua, reprinted in Women of China (Online), 5 June 07.
²⁷ "Report: Unsafe Sex Major Cause of HIV Infection," China Daily (Online), 20 August 07.
²⁸ CECC, 2003 Annual Report, 49.
²⁹ "China's Suicide Rate Among World's Highest," China Daily (Online), 11 September 07; Christopher Allen, "Traditions Weigh on China's Women," BBC (Online), 20 June 06; World

Health Organization, "Suicide Huge but Preventable Public Health Problem," 10 September 04; Maureen Fan, "In Rural China, a Bitter Way out," Washington Post (Online), 15 May 07.

[30] "Domestic Violence is the Main Reason Chinese Rural Women Commit Suicide" [Jiating baoli shi daozhi zhongguo nongcun funü zisha de zhuyin], Radio Free Asia (Online), 28 November 06; CECC, 2006 Annual Report, 99; Fan, "In Rural China, a Bitter Way out."

[31] Over the period from 1991 to 2004, "national statistics show[ed] an overall decline in maternal mortality from 80 to 48.3 deaths per 100,000 live births." There is a divide between urban and rural areas, however, as the maternal mortality rate in small and medium cities had declined to 15.3 deaths per 100,000 live births by 2004, compared to 96 deaths per 100,000 in remote rural areas. The gap has widened since 1996. China Development Brief (Online), "Drop in Maternal and Child Mortality Slow and Uneven," 18 January 07.

[32] Human Rights in China, "Implementation of the Convention of the Elimination of All Forms of Discrimination Against Women in the People's Republic of China," 15.

[33] A 2005 report by China Children's Center reported 99.14 percent enrollment rates for girls, and 99.16 percent enrollment rates for boys. "Girls and Boys have Basically the Same Rate of Entry into School," Xinhua (Online), 9 December 06. See also, China Statistical Yearbook 2006, Figure 21–5 titled "Number of New Students Enrollment by Level and Type of School."

[34] "China Still Has 100 Million Illiterate People; Of that, 70% are Women" [Wuguo haiyou wenmang 1 yi duo qizhong nüxing yu qicheng], People's Daily (Online), 17 October 06; The State Council Women's Development Program, 2001–2010.

[35] "Spring Bud Program Helps 2622 Girls Stay in School over 11 Years in Ningxia" ["Chunlei nainai" jianglijuan: 11 nian zizhu 2622 ming shixue nütong], Xinhua (Online), 14 November 06; "'Spring Bud Program' Helps 1,600,000 Girls Return to School" ["Chunlei jihua" bang 160 wan nütong chongfan xiaoyuan], China Women's News (Online), 18 October 06.

[36] Xulin and Sun Xiaosu, "Married-out Women in Guangdong Province Gain Hope."

[37] Ibid.; "Women Sue Village Committees for Denying Them Land Rights," CECC China Human Rights and Rule of Law Update, July 2006, 8.

[38] Xulin and Sun Xiaosu, "Married-out Women in Guangdong Province Gain Hope."

[39] Ibid.

[40] PRC Organic Law of Village Committees, enacted 4 November 98, art. 20. Article 20 states that "no villagers charter of self-government, rules and regulations for the village, villagers pledges or matters decided through discussions by a villagers assembly or by representatives of villagers may contravene the Constitution, laws, regulations, or State policies, or contain such contents as infringing upon villagers rights of the person, their democratic rights or lawful property rights."

[41] Xulin and Sun Xiaosu, "Married-out Women in Guangdong Province Gain Hope."

[42] Ibid.

[43] Ibid.

[44] CECC Staff Interview; Xu Yushan, "A Preliminary Analysis of the Relationship between the Women's Federation and Other Women's Organizations" [Qianxi fulian yu qita funüzuzhi de guanxi], Collection of Women's Studies [Funü yanjiu luncong], No. 2, March 2004, 44–48.

[45] China Women's University established a legal center for women and children in September 2006 that offers free legal services primarily to women and children, but also to other "vulnerable groups" such as the elderly and the disabled. Legal services include counseling over the telephone, counseling in person, drafting documents on behalf of someone else, mediation, and litigation. "China Women's University Establishes Legal Center for Women and Children" [Zhonghua nüzi xueyuan chengli funü ertong falü fuwu zhongxin], China Women's News, reprinted in Women Watch—China (Online), 26 September 06. In September 2006, the Beijing Lawyers Association Marriage and Family Special Committee held a seminar that focused on legal protections of women's land rights, seminars are held to brainstorm questions and raise suggestions to the Legislation Department, regarding the land rights and interests of women, especially married-out women, divorced women, and widows. "Seminar on Legal Protection of Women's Land Rights" [Tudi yong yi quan falü shiwu wenti yantaohui], Women Watch—China (Online), 1 October 06.

[46] CECC, 2006 Annual Report, 98.

[47] Ibid., 98.

[48] CECC, 2005 Annual Report, 72.

[49] "Chinese Villages Have Roughly 47 Million 'Left Behind Women'" [Zhongguo nongcun "liushou funü" yue 4700 wan], Radio Free Asia (Online), 8 November 06.

[50] "Older Pregnant Woman Unexpectedly Dismissed by Company" [Gaoling bailing huaiyun jing bei gongsi jiegu], New Express, reprinted in Women Watch—China (Online), 3 November 06.

[51] The survey data was collected from 6,595 questionnaires handed out in 416 villages and four cities. "Female Migrants Suffering at Work," China Daily, 30 November 06 (Open Source Center, 30 November 06).

[52] Liu Yun and Yao Jian, "Legal Aid for Female Migrant Workers," China Women's News, reprinted in Women Watch—China (Online), 21 June 07.

[53] Ibid.

[54] "Over 60 Million Female Workers Have Maternity Insurance," Women of China (Online), 21 June 07. The Yunnan Provincial Health Bureau launched a project to raise public awareness of HIV/AIDS, with the aim of educating 80 percent of its female population. "Project Launched To Protect Women from AIDS," China News (Online), 13 July 07. Some local governments have established programs to provide loans and training to women who have lost their jobs. Liu Yun and Yao Jian, "Legal Aid for Female Migrant Workers."

[55] "Why Can't Women Retire at the Same Age as Men" [Nüren pingsha wuquan yu nanren tongling tuixiu], Southern Weekend (Online), 13 October 05.

[56] "Why Can't Women Retire at the Same Age as Men," Southern Weekend; CECC, 2005 Annual Report, 67.

[57] "Hubei Transportation Company: Female Attendants Whose Weight Exceeds 60 Kilograms Must Step Down" [Nü chengwuyuan tizhong chaoguo 60 gongjin jiang xiagang], Radio Free Asia (Online), 7 October 06.

[58] China Gender Equality and Women's Development Report [Zhongguo xingbie pingdeng yu funü fazhan baogao], ed. Tan Lin (Beijing: Social Sciences Academic Press, 2006), reprinted in China Net (Online).

Notes to Section II—Population Planning

[1] CECC, 2006 Annual Report, 20 September 06, 109.

[2] The population increased by roughly 300 million from 1980 to 2005. Statistic cited in Tyrene White, China's Longest Campaign: Birth Planning in the People's Republic, 1949–2005 (Ithaca: Cornell UP, 2006), 263. For official Chinese government information on its population planning policies see State Council Information Office, White Paper on Population in China, 19 December 00. For information on the number of births prevented, see paragraph 7 of the report.

[3] Quoted in White, China's Longest Campaign, 238.

[4] Central Committee of the CCP and State Council Decision Regarding the Comprehensive Strengthening of Population and Family Planning Work To Resolve the Population Problem as a Whole [Zhonggong zhongyang guowuyuan guanyu quanmian jiaqiang renkou he jihua shengyu gongzuo tongchou jiejue renkou wenti de jueding], issued 17 December 06.

[5] Guan Xiaofeng, "Official: Family Planning Policy To Stay," China Daily, reprinted on the National Population and Family Planning Commission of China Web site, 4 July 07.

[6] The circumstances under which women may bear a second child are governed by provincial-level regulations. Provincial regulations have allowed additional children for ethnic minorities and some rural Han Chinese residents and permitted second births where the first child is a girl, is disabled, or, in some cases, where both parents are only children themselves, among other circumstances. For basic codification of the one-child policy, see Population and Family Planning Law of the People's Republic of China (Population and Family Planning Law), adopted 29 December 01, art. 18. For examples of restrictions in local regulations, see, e.g., Henan Province Population and Family Planning Regulation [Henansheng renkou yu jihua shengyu tiaoli], adopted 30 November 02, art. 15, 17, 18; Xinjiang Uighur Autonomous Region (XUAR) Regulation on Population and Family Planning [Xinjiang weiwu'er zizhiqu renkou yu jihua shengyu tiaoli], art. 15. Article 15 of the Henan province regulation "advocates that a couple give birth to one child, strictly controls the birth of a second child, and prohibits the birth of a third child." Articles 17 and 18 stipulate conditions under which couples may apply for approval to have a second child, such as where a first child carries a genetic disability. Article 15 of the XUAR regulation allows urban Han Chinese couples to have one child, urban ethnic minority couples and rural Han Chinese couples to have two, and rural ethnic minority couples to have three. See also Gu Baochang et al., "China's Local and National Fertility Policies at the End of the Twentieth Century," Population and Development Review 33(1), March 2007, 132–136. Government officials have attempted to downplay controls by stating that a strict one-child rule affects less than 36 percent of the population. See, e.g., "Many Free To Have More Than One Child," Xinhua (Online), 11 July 07.

[7] Population and Family Planning Law, art. 41. Each provincial-level government determines its own fees. Measures for Collection of Social Compensation Fees [Shehui fuyangfei zhengshou guanli banfa], issued 2 September 02, art. 3, 7. In Beijing, parents who have children in violation of the local regulation, including unmarried women who are in violation by giving birth to a child, face fines that range from 3 to 10 times the area's average income. Beijing Measures for Managing the Collection of Social Compensation Fees [Beijing shi shehui fuyangfei zhengshou guanli banfa], adopted 5 November 02, art. 5. Fees are lower in Shandong province, where the fine is set at 30 percent of local incomes. Shandong Province Measures for Managing the Collection of Birth Control Social Compensation Fees [Shandongsheng jihua shengyu shehui fuyangfei zhengshou guanli banfa], issued 1998, art. 4.

[8] Bureau of Democracy, Human Rights, and Labor, U.S. Department of State, Country Reports on Human Rights Practices—2006, China (includes Tibet, Hong Kong, and Macau) (Online), 6 March 07.

[9] Under Article 41 of the Population and Family Planning Law, where a citizen does not pay the social compensation fee, "the administrative department for family planning that makes the decision on collection of the fees shall, in accordance with law, apply to the People's Court for enforcement." Population and Family Planning Law, art. 41. U.S. Department of State, Country Reports on Human Rights Practices—2006; CECC Staff Interview.

[10] See, e.g., "Family Planning Faces Challenge from New Rich," Xinhua, reprinted in China Daily (Online), 14 December 05. Officials have said the government will take measures to discourage wealthier citizens from violating restrictions. Alice Yan and Kristine Kwok, "One-Child Crackdown Looms for Elite; Officials Consider Stiffer Penalties for Rich and Famous Who Flout Family Policy," South China Morning Post (Online), 1 March 07.

[11] "2,000 Officials Breach 'One-Child' Policy in Hunan," China Daily, reprinted on China Elections and Governance Web site, 9 July 07. The Hunan government amended local regulations on population planning in September to increase fines for violating the regulations. "Chinese Province Raises Fines on Wealthy Flouters of Family Planning Laws," Xinhua, 29 September 07 (Open Source Center, 29 September 07).

[12] "Chinese Officials Breaching One-Child Policy Denied Promotion," Xinhua, 14 September 07 (Open Source Center, 14 September 07).

[13] See, e.g., "State Population and Family Planning Commission Indicates 'Encouraging and Rewarding Fewer Births' To Be Carried Out at Least 20–30 Years" [Guojia renkou jishengwei biaoshi "jiangli shaosheng" zhishao zhixing er san shinian], People's Daily (Online), 19 October 06; "Encouragement and Reward Assistance System To Enter Implementation Phase" [Jiangli fuzhu zhidu jiang jinru shishi jieduan], People's Daily (Online), 16 October 06. Yang Jie, "Auton-

omous Region Launches Important Reform on General College Entrance Examination," Xinjiang Daily, 31 May 07 (Open Source Center, 12 June 07).

[14] National Population and Family Planning Commission Circular on Printing and Distributing Action Plan for Special Rectification of Unlawful Births in Cities and Towns [Guojia renkou jishengwei guanyu yinfa chengzhen weifa shengyu zhuanxiang zhili xingdong fang'an de tongzhi], issued 24 May 07. For an English translation, see "China: Action Plan To Rectify Unlawful Births in Urban Areas," Open Source Center, 16 June 07.

[15] Convention on the Elimination of All Forms of Discrimination Against Women, adopted and opened for signature, ratification, and accession by General Assembly resolution 34/180 of 18 December 79, entry into force 3 September 81, art. 2, 3, 16(1)(e).

[16] Convention on the Rights of the Child, adopted and opened for signature, ratification, and accession by General Assembly resolution 44/25 of 20 November 89, entry into force 2 September 90, art. 2, 3, 4, 6, 26. China has submitted a reservation to Article 6: "[T]he People's Republic of China shall fulfil its obligations provided by article 6 of the Convention under the prerequisite that the Convention accords with the provisions of article 25 concerning family planning of the Constitution of the People's Republic of China and in conformity with the provisions of article 2 of the Law of Minor Children of the People's Republic of China." Office of the UN High Commissioner for Human Rights, "Declarations and reservations to the Convention on the Rights of the Child" (Online).

[17] International Covenant on Economic, Social, and Cultural Rights (ICESCR) adopted by General Assembly resolution 2200 A (XXI) of 16 December 66, entry into force 3 January 76, art. 10(3).

[18] Population and Family Planning Law, art. 39.

[19] See, e.g., "7,000 Forcibly Sterilised in Eastern China," South China Morning Post (Online), 12 September 05; Joseph Kahn, "Advocate for China's Weak Crosses the Powerful," New York Times, 20 July 06. For Chinese reporting on events in Linyi, see, e.g., "Officials Fired for Forced Abortions," Xinhua (Online), 21 September 05; "PRC Official Confirms Irregularities in Shandong Family Planning Management," Xinhua, 19 September 05 (Open Source Center, 26 September 05).

[20] See the CECC Political Prisoner Database for more information on Chen Guangcheng.

[21] See, e.g., "Guangxi Town 'Tense' After One-Child Protest Put Down," South China Morning Post (Online), 22 May 07; Joseph Kahn, "Birth Control Measures Prompt Riots in China," New York Times (Online), 21 May 07; "Government Uses Iron Fist To Force Sterilization of Female Student" [Zhengfu tiewan bi nüsheng jueyu], Ming Pao (Online), 22 May 07.

[22] See, e.g., Chow Chung-yan, "One-Child Policy Riots Flare Up—Anger Over Birth-Control Fines Spreads across Guangxi," South China Morning Post (Online), 31 May 07; "10,000 Riot in Guangxi," Tung Fang Jih Pao, 21 May 07 (Open Source Center, 21 May 07); "Guangxi Family Planning Protests Erupt Again in Rong County," Radio Free Asia (Online), 29 May 07. In July, state-controlled media reported that two men received prisons sentences of one and two years for their involvement in the protests. "China Jails Two Men for Birth-Control Riots," Reuters (Online), 23 July 07.

[23] "Full-Term Abortion Lawsuit a First for China," Caijing (Online), 25 July 07.

[24] The pressures created by population planning policies, combined with entrenched preferences for male children and under-reporting of female births, have factored into estimates of China's unbalanced sex ratio. See White, China's Longest Campaign, 203–207, for more information on sex ratios in China and in other countries with traditional preferences for boys.

[25] "New Policy Will Offer Cash Instead of Kids," China Daily (Online), 16 October 06.

[26] Decision Regarding the Comprehensive Strengthening of Population and Family Planning Work To Resolve the Population Problem as a Whole. Article 35 of the 2002 Population and Family Planning Law prohibits, but does not penalize, sex-selective abortion. Population and Family Planning Law, art. 35.

[27] Statistics cited in U.S. Department of State, "Country Reports on Human Rights Practices—2006. There is some variation in reporting on the sex ratio. See the CECC, 2006 Annual Report, 230 (footnote 34) for an overview of estimates during and before 2006.

[28] "Abortion Law Amendment To Be Abolished," China Daily, reprinted in Xinhua, 26 June 06.

[29] Henan Province Regulation on Prohibiting Non-Medically Necessary Fetal Sex Determination and Sex-Selective Abortion [Henansheng jinzhi feiyixue xuyao tai'er xingbie jianding he xuenze xingbie rengong zhongzhi renshen tiaoli], issued 29 September 06. The regulation only allows sex determination for cases in which medical personnel suspect the existence of a congenital disease. For women who have abided by all population planning requirements and are more than 14 weeks pregnant, abortion is permitted only when a serious hereditary disease or severe birth defect is detected; if continuation of gestation will damage the health or life of the pregnant woman; or if the pregnant woman is divorced or widowed. The regulation does not alter the legal framework for abortion prior to 14 weeks of gestation or for women whose pregnancy violates population planning requirements. The regulation also prohibits the retail sale of abortion-inducing drugs, limits manufacturers' ability to distribute such pharmaceuticals, and requires a physician to administer these drugs. Penalties include fines of up to 2,000 yuan (US$260) for women who have abortions in violation of the regulation's parameters, and fines of up to 30,000 yuan (US$3,870) and possible revocation of licenses for health organizations that do not comply with the new regulation.

[30] For an overview of such measures, known as a "1.5-children policy," see Gu, "China's Local and National Fertility Policies at the End of the Twentieth Century," 133, 138.

[31] Office to Monitor and Combat Trafficking in Persons, U.S. Department of State, Trafficking in Persons Report—China, 12 June 07.

[32] "Xinjiang Focuses on Reducing Births in Minority Areas To Curb Population Growth," CECC China Human Rights and Rule of Law Update, April 2006, 15–16; "Xinjiang Reports High Rate of Population Increase," CECC China Human Rights and Rule of Law Update, March 2006,

16–17. A 1953 government census found that Han Chinese constituted 6 percent of the XUAR's population of 4.87 million, while Uighurs made up 75 percent. The 2000 census listed the Han population at 40.57 percent and Uighurs at 45.21 percent of a total population of 18.46 million. Demographer Stanley Toops has noted that Han migration since the 1950s is responsible for the "bulk" of the XUAR's high population growth in the past half century. Stanley Toops, "Demographics and Development in Xinjiang after 1949,"East-West Center Washington Working Papers No. 1, May 04, 1.

Notes to Section II—Health
[1] Beijing Municipality Regulations on Mental Health [Beijing shi jingshen weisheng tiaoli], issued 8 December 06. According to a 2002 Human Rights Watch report, while an international delegation visited Beijing in 1993 as part of China's bid for the 2000 Olympics, individuals with mental illnesses were removed from the streets and housed in temporary holding centers. Human Rights Watch (Online), "Dangerous Minds, Political Psychiatry in China Today and its Origins in the Mao Era," August 2002.
[2] Beijing Municipality Regulations on Mental Health, art. 31.
[3] G.A. Res. 119, U.N. GAOR, 46th Sess., Supp. No. 49, Annex, at 188–192, U.N. Doc. A/46/49 (1991). The General Assembly approved this resolution without a vote on December 17, 1991. The resolution is not binding and it is unclear whether China supported it. Beijing's mental health regulations, however, include a number of provisions that are similar to those found in the Principles, suggesting that officials modeled their provisions in part on the Principles.
[4] Beijing Municipality Regulations on Mental Health, arts. 27, 32.
[5] "Progress in AIDS Battle despite Harassment," Reuters, reprinted in South China Morning Post (Online), 18 July 07.
[6] Ibid.
[7] The Center for Strategic and International Studies, "Averting a Full-Blown HIV/AIDS Epidemic in China: A Report of the CSIS HIV/AIDS Delegation in China, 13–17 January 2003," February 2003, 2; United Nations Theme Group of HIV/AIDS in China, "HIV/AIDS: China's Titanic Peril-2001 Update of the AIDS Situation and Needs Assessment Report," June 2002, 7.
[8] The Center for Strategic and International Studies, "Demography of HIV/AIDS in China: A Report of the Task Force on HIV/AIDS," July 2007, 10.
[9] "Progress in AIDS Battle despite Harassment," Reuters.
[10] "China reports leap in new HIV/AIDS cases," Reuters (Online), 9 September 07.
[11] "New Estimate in China Finds Fewer AIDS Cases," New York Times (Online), 26 January 06.
[12] "Progress in AIDS Battle despite Harassment," Reuters; "UNAIDS Chief Sees Signs of Progress in China," Reuters, reprinted in Yahoo! (Online), 17 July 07.
[13] Evelyn Iritani, "China's AIDS Battle Goes Corporate," Los Angeles Times (Online), 3 March 07.
[14] Ibid.
[15] Ibid.
[16] Ben Blanchard, "China Not Investing Enough To Fight AIDS: Experts," Reuters, 5 April 07. As Thomas Cai, founder of AIDS Care China, notes: "Initial progress was made in Beijing because people in the ministries were working with U.N. people and the international community. When you get down to the lower level, people still have a different mind-set." Iritani, "China's AIDS Battle Goes Corporate."
[17] "Hundreds of Police Storm 'AIDS Village' in China, Arrest 13 Farmers," Agence France-Presse (Online), 3 July 03.
[18] Chan Siu-sin, "Four Residents of Henan AIDS Village Obstructed from Petitioning Beijing," South China Morning Post (Online), 4 July 04.
[19] Human Rights Watch, Restrictions on AIDS Activists in China, June 2005, 19; International Federation for Human Rights, Alternative Report to the Committee on Economic, Social and Cultural Rights: China: 'At a Critical Stage,' Violations of the Right to Health in the Context of the Fight against AIDS, April 2005.
[20] "AIDS Activist Resigns from Civil Society Organization, Cites Government Pressure," CECC China Human Rights and Rule of Law Update, March 2006, 7–8; "Progress in AIDS Battle despite Harassment," Reuters.
[21] "Beijing PSB Officials Hold AIDS Activist Wan Yanhai, Cancel AIDS Conference," CECC China Human Rights and Rule of Law Update, December 2006, 8–9.
[22] Jim Yardley, "Detained AIDS Doctor Allowed To Visit U.S. Later, China Says," New York Times (Online), 17 February 07.
[23] Ibid.
[24] Minnie Chan, "Blood Centre Boss Fired, Six Jailed over Illegal Sales," South China Morning Post (Online), 11 July 07.
[25] Shan Juan, "Blood Collections To Be Videotaped," China Daily (Online), 11 July 07.
[26] Dune Lawrence, "China's Lack of HIV/AIDS Awareness Undermines Control Program," Bloomberg (Online), 9 April 07. In addition, an UNAIDS report released in March 2006 found that China was only half way to meeting its goal under the UN's "3 by 5" initiative of providing 30,000 HIV/AIDS carriers access to anti-HIV/AIDS drugs by the end of 2005. World Health Organization and UNAIDS, "Progress on Global Access to HIV Antiretroviral Therapy: A Report on 3 by 5 and Beyond," 28 March 06, 72; CECC, 2006 Annual Report, 20 September 06, 111.
[27] "Number of Tibetans with HIV/AIDS Rising" [Xizang HIV/AIDS renshu shangsheng], Radio Free Asia (Online), 17 June 07; Bill Savadove, "140,000 Orphaned by AIDS, Says UNICEF," South China Morning Post (Online), 9 July 07.
[28] Iritani, "China's AIDS Battle Goes Corporate."
[29] Lawrence, "China's Lack of HIV/AIDS Awareness Undermines Control Program;" "Discrimination against HIV Patients Still Rife," Xinhua, reprinted in China.org (Online), 29 November 06.

[30] "5-Year-old AIDS Patient Denied Surgery by Guangdong Hospitals" [Aizi nantong qiuyi zaoju] Southern Metropolitan Daily (Online), 25 June 07; Chinese Human Rights Defenders (Online), "Minquan County AIDS Patients Encounter Unfair Treatment at Police Station" [Minquan aizibing ren zaodao paichusuo de bugong daiyu], 5 July 07.

[31] "Doctors Not Up to Scratch on Hepatitis," China Daily (Online), 29 September 05; Bonny Ling and Wing Lam, "Hepatitis B: A Catalyst for Anti-Discrimination Reforms?," 2 China Rights Forum 67, 68 (2007).

[32] Ministry of Health (Online), "Ministry of Health Publishes '2006–2010 Plan on Hepatitis B Prevention and Control'" ["2006–2010 nian quanguo yi xing bingduxing ganyan fangzhi guihua" fabu], 13 February 06.

[33] CECC, 2004 Annual Report, 5 October 04, 65.

[34] "Law To Protect HB Virus Carriers," China Daily (Online), 24 August 04.

[35] "Plaintiff Wins Nominally in the First Hepatitis B Discrimination Lawsuit" ['Yigan qishi diyian' yuangao mingyi shang huosheng], Beijing Youth Daily (Online), 3 April 04.

[36] PRC Law on the Prevention and Control of Infectious Diseases, enacted 29 February 89, amended 28 August 04; CECC, 2004 Annual Report, 61.

[37] Zhang Feng, "HBV Victims Face Improved Job Chances," China Daily (Online), 19 January 05; "Public Opinion Defeats HBV Discrimination," China Internet Information Center (Online), 23 September 04.

[38] Vivien Cui, "Hepatitis B Carriers Forced To Suffer in Silence," South China Morning Post (Online), 5 September 06; "Xinjiang Hepatitis Students Fight School Ban," Radio Free Asia (Online), 20 November 06.

[39] "Doctors Not Up to Scratch on Hepatitis," China Daily.

[40] China Development Brief (Online), "Hepatitis Foundation Learns from AIDS Activism," 16 February 06.

[41] Ibid.; "Xinjiang First Hepatitis B Discrimination Case Docketed, Incoming Student Sues Xinjiang Agricultural University [Xinjiang shou li yigan qishi an lian xiuxue xinsheng zhuanggao nongye daxue]," City Consumer Morning News (Online), 29 January 06.

[42] China Development Brief (Online), "Hepatitis B Stigma Provokes Outcry in Xinjiang," 30 October 06; "Xinjiang First Hepatitis B Discrimination Case Docketed, Incoming Student Sues Xinjiang Agricultural University," City Consumer Morning News.

[43] "December 16, Friday, Plaintiff in First Hepatitis B Discrimination Case in Xinjiang Successfully Resumes Student Status" [12 yue 16 ri, xingqiwu, xinjiang yigan qishi di yi dan dangshiren liyi shunli bu ban qiquan xueji], Boxun (Online), 18 December 06.

[44] China Development Brief, "Hepatitis B Stigma Provokes Outcry in Xinjiang;" Mure Dickie, "Parents in Xinjiang Drop Discrimination Suit," Financial Times (Online), 18 September 07; "Xinjiang Hepatitis Students Fight School Ban," Radio Free Asia; "7 Hepatitis B-Positive Chinese Students Sue," Associated Press, reprinted in China Daily (Online), 23 October 07.

[45] Ibid.

[46] China Development Brief, "Hepatitis B Stigma Provokes Outcry in Xinjiang;" "Xinjiang Hepatitis Students Fight School Ban," Radio Free Asia.

[47] Ibid.

[48] Ibid.; Mure Dickie, "Parents in Xinjiang Drop Discrimination Suit;" "7 Hepatitis B-Positive Chinese Students Sue," Associated Press.

[49] "Xinjiang Hepatitis Students Fight School Ban," Radio Free Asia.

[50] "Survey Shows Half of Chinese Discriminate against People with HIV/AIDS" [Mintiao xianshi duoban zhongguoren paichi aizibingren], Voice of America (Online), 14 May 07.

[51] Xin Dingding, "Law To Protect Hepatitis B Carriers' Rights," China Daily (Online), 14 July 07.

[52] Mure Dickie, "Nokia China Hit with Discrimination Suit," Financial Times (Online), 13 March 07.

[53] "Nokia Hepatitis B Discrimination Case Will Open in Court on August 9, People are Welcome To Attend" [Nokia yigan qishi an jiang yu 8 yue 9 ri kaiting, huanying canjia pangting, caifang], Boxun (Online), 3 August 07; "Nokia China Faces Lawsuit over Rejection of Hepatitis-B Carrier," Helsingin Sanomat (Online), 16 August 07.

[54] Ibid.; "August 15 Dongguan Nokia Employment Discrimination Case Outcome and Situation Report from the Plaintiff's Lawyer" [8 yue 15 ri dongguan nuojiya jiuye qishi anjian shenpan jieguo yiji yu wofang lüshi jiaoliu qingkuang huibao], Gandan Xiangzhao (Online), 15 August 07.

[55] CECC Staff Search. See also, "August 15 Dongguan Nokia Employment Discrimination Case Outcome and Situation Report from the Plaintiff's Lawyer," Gandan Xiangzhao.

[56] Chinese Human Rights Defenders (Online), "Government Issues New Regulations Protecting the Employment Rights of Hepatitis B Carriers" [Guanfang chuxin gui yaoqiu weihu yigan biaomian kangyuan xiedaizhe jiuye quanli], 31 May 07; Bonny Ling and Wing Lam, "Hepatitis B: A Catalyst for Anti-Discrimination Reforms?," 2 China Rights Forum 67, 72–73 (2007).

[57] "New Law Allows Job Seekers To Litigate Against Discrimination," Xinhua (Online), 30 August 07; Xin Dingding, "Law To Protect Hepatitis B Carriers' Rights."

[58] PRC Employment Promotion Law, enacted 30 August 07, arts. 30, 62; "A Call for NGO Colleagues to Pay Attention to the Employment Promotion Law Anti-Discrimination Provision that Leaves out Discrimination against Carriers of Hepatitis B and HIV" [Huyu NGO tongren guanzhu "jiuye cujin fa" fei qishi tiaokuan yilou yigan he aizi qishi wenti], Boxun (Online), 2 March 07.

[59] "Legislation for Anti-Discrimination in Employment Urgently Needed" [Fan yigan jiuye qishi ying lifa], China Youth Daily (Online), 5 February 07; Bonny Ling and Wing Lam, "Hepatitis B: A Catalyst for Anti-Discrimination Reforms?," 2 China Rights Forum 67, 71 (2007).

[60] Xin Dingding, "Law To Protect Hepatitis B Carriers' Rights."

[61] "SARS Whistle-Blower Barred from US Prize Trip," Agence France-Presse, reprinted in South China Morning Post (Online), 12 July 07.

[62] Emergency Response Regulations for Major Epidemics of Animal Diseases [Zhongda dongwu yiqing yingji tiaoli], issued 18 November 05, Ch. 3, art. 17.

[63] Human Rights in China (Online), "State Secrets: China's Legal Labyrinth," June 2007, 180.

[64] Regulation of the People's Republic of China on the Public Disclosure of Government Information [Zhonghua renmin gongheguo zhengfu xinxi gongkai tiaoli], issued 5 April 07, art. 14.

[65] Cao Haidong and Fu Jianfeng, "20 Years of Health Care Reform in China" [Zhongguo yigai 20 nian], Southern Daily (Online), 5 August 05; Ofra Anson and Shifang Sun, Health Care in Rural China (Ashgate, Aldershot, Hants, 2005), 15–17.

[66] Yuanli Liu, "Development of the Rural Health Insurance System in China," Health Policy and Planning, 19(3), 2004, 160.

[67] "Residents of Chinese Cities Live on Average 12 Years Longer than Those in Rural Areas—What Is the Cause?" [Zhongguo dachengshi renjun shouming bi nongcun gao 12 nian—shi he yuanyin?], Xinhua (Online), 17 November 05.

[68] "Facts and Figures: Widening Gap between China's Urban, Rural Areas," People's Daily (Online), 3 March 06.

[69] "Residents of Chinese Cities Live on Average 12 Years Longer than Those in Rural Areas-What Is the Cause?," Xinhua.

[70] "National Healthcare Needs Gradual Growth," China Daily (Online), 26 March 07.

[71] "China will Augment Basic Urban Healthcare Insurance," Xinhua, reprinted in China.org (Online), 25 July 07.

[72] "Premier Wen Sees How Urban Medicare Works," Xinhua, reprinted in China Daily (Online), 22 July 07.

[73] David Blumenthal and William Hsiao, "Privatization and its Discontents—The Evolving Chinese Health Care System," 353 New England Journal of Medicine 1165, 1169 (2005); CECC, 2006 Annual Report, 109.

[74] "Rural Medical System Covers Nearly Half of Farmers," Xinhua, reprinted in China.org (Online), 11 September 06; "National Healthcare Needs Gradual Growth," China Daily.

[75] "Rural Medical System Covers Nearly Half of Farmers," Xinhua; "Healthcare Plans in Pipeline," China Daily, reprinted in China.org (Online), 12 March 07.

[76] Duncan Hewitt, "China Rural Health Worries," BBC News (Online), 4 July 02.

[77] "China Rebuilding Rural Cooperative Medicare System," Xinhua, reprinted in Beijing Review (Online), 21 February 07.

[78] "Healthcare Plans in Pipeline," China Daily; "Gov't under Pressure To Make Rural Healthcare System Work," Xinhua, reprinted in China.org (Online), 21 April 07.

[79] "Rural Medical System Covers Nearly Half of Farmers," Xinhua; "Rural Cooperative Healthcare Network Planned [sic]," Xinhua, reprinted in China.org (Online), 8 June 07.

[80] "Half of All Farmers Do Not Seek Care for Illness" [Zhongguo nongmin yiban kanbuqi bing], Beijing News (Online), 6 November 04; "Half of All Children Who Die of Illness in the Countryside Had Not Received Medical Treatment" [Wo guo yin bing siwang de nongcun ertong reng you yibanwei dedao yiliao], People's Daily (Online), 17 August 05; CECC, 2005 Annual Report, 11 October 05, 72.

[81] "Gov't under Pressure To Make Rural Healthcare System Work," Xinhua.

[82] "China Rebuilding Rural Cooperative Medicare System," Xinhua.

[83] "Survey: Medical Expenses Account for 11.8% of Family's Annual Spending," Yahoo!, translated on the Web site of Women of China, 26 December 06.

[84] "Doctors Face Growing Risk of Violent Medical Disputes," Xinhua, reprinted in China.org (Online), 18 April 07.

[85] Ibid.

[86] "Rural Cooperative Healthcare Network Planned [sic]," Xinhua.

[87] "Rural Medical System Covers Nearly Half of Farmers," Xinhua.

Notes to Section II—Human Trafficking

[1] Office to Monitor and Combat Trafficking in Persons, U.S. Department of State, Trafficking in Persons Report—China, 12 June 07, 80.

[2] PRC Protection of Minors Law, enacted 4 September 91, amended 29 December 06.

[3] Ibid., art. 41.

[4] "More Forced into Labor, Prostitution," China Daily (Online), 27 July 07.

[5] National Bureau of Statistics, China Statistical Yearbook 2006, Table 23–11; "Ministry of Public Security Strengthens the Combating of Crimes of Trafficking in Women and Children" [Zhongguo gongan jiguan jiada daji guaimai funü ertong fanzui lidu], Xinhua (Online), 26 July 07.

[6] U.S. Department of State, Trafficking in Persons Report—China, 80.

[7] "More Forced into Labor, Prostitution," China Daily.

[8] Experts believe that Chinese law only considers those under the age of 14 to be "minors" and automatic victims of trafficking, with no need for personnel to have them examined for signs of coercion or the use of force. CECC Staff Correspondence; "Ministry of Public Security Official: Human Trafficking for the Purposes of Forced Labor and Sexual Exploitation Has Increased" [Gonganbu guanyuan: yi boxue he seqing wei mudi de renkou guaimai shangsheng], China Daily, reprinted in China Economic Net (Online), 27 July 07. See, for example, the PRC Criminal Law, enacted 1 July 79, amended 14 March 97, 25 December 99, 31 August 01, 29 December 01, 28 December 02, 28 February 05, 29 June 06, art. 240.

[9] UNICEF (Online), "China: Trafficking of Children and Women," last visited 4 October 07; "China To Issue An Anti-Trafficking Plan" [Zhongguo jiang zhiding guojia fan renkou guaimai xingdong jihua], Xinhua (Online), 12 July 06.

[10] U.S. Department of State, Trafficking in Persons Report—China, 80.

[11] Ibid.

[12] CECC Staff Correspondence.

[13] UNICEF, "China: Trafficking of Children and Women;" "China To Issue An Anti-Trafficking Plan," Xinhua; "Hunan Court Sentences Infant Traffickers; New Orphanage Standards Due Soon," CECC China Human Rights and Rule of Law Update, April 2006, 3–4; "Social Service Organizations Involved in Two Child Trafficking Cases," CECC China Human Rights and Rule of Law Update, January 2006, 11; Bureau of Democracy, Human Rights, and Labor, U.S. Department of State, Country Reports on Human Rights Practices—2006, China (includes Tibet, Hong Kong, and Macau), 6 March 07, sec. 5.

[14] U.S. Department of State, Country Reports on Human Rights Practices—2006, China, sec. 5.

[15] "Social Service Organizations Involved in Two Child Trafficking Cases," CECC China Human Rights and Rule of Law Update, 11; "Hunan Court Sentences Infant Traffickers; New Orphanage Standards Due Soon," CECC China Human Rights and Rule of Law Update, 3–4; Cindy Sui, "Baby Trafficking in PRC's Rural Areas 'Widespread,'" Agence France-Presse, 5 February 05 (Open Source Center, 10 February 05).

[16] U.S. Department of State, Trafficking in Persons Report—China, 80.

[17] United Nations Office on Drugs and Crime (Online), "The United Nations Convention Against Transnational Organized Crime and Its Protocols," last viewed 4 October 07; UN Convention Against Transnational Organized Crime, adopted by General Assembly resolution 55/25 of 15 November 2000, entry into force 29 September 03; Protocol to Prevent, Suppress and Punish Trafficking in Persons, Especially Women and Children (commonly known as Palermo Protocol), adopted by General Assembly resolution 55/25 of 15 November 2000, entry into force on 25 December 03.

[18] Convention on the Elimination of All Forms of Discrimination Against Women, adopted by General Assembly resolution 34/180 of 18 December 79, entry into force 3 September 81, art. 6; Convention on the Rights of the Child, adopted by the General Assembly resolution 44/25 of 20 November 1989, entry into force 2 September 90, art. 35; Human Trafficking.org (Online), "Government of China's Plan of Action To Prevent, Protect, Prosecute and Reintegrate," last viewed 4 October 07.

[19] PRC Law on the Protection of Women's Rights and Interests, enacted 3 April 92, amended 28 August 05, art. 39.

[20] "China To Issue a National Anti-Trafficking Plan of Action," Xinhua (Online), 12 July 06; "Panel Set To Target Human Trafficking," China Daily (Online), 4 September 07.

[21] For example, the Ministry of Justice launched a three month campaign in 2000 that reportedly resulted in the rescue of some 10,000 girls. CECC, 2003 Annual Report, 2 October 03, 53. From 2001 to 2003, the Ministry of Public Security initiated a series of "Strike Hard" campaigns that reportedly solved 20,360 cases involving 42,215 victims. CECC, 2004 Annual Report, 5 October 04, 137, endnote 527.

[22] Murray Scot Tanner, "State Coercion and the Balance of Awe: The 1983–1986 'Stern Blows' Anti-Crime Campaign," China Journal, July 2000.

[23] Office to Monitor and Combat Trafficking in Persons, U.S. Department of State, Trafficking in Persons Interim Assessment—China, 19 January 07.

[24] Ibid.

[25] Ibid.

[26] U.S. Department of State, Trafficking in Persons Report—China, 80; "Social Service Organizations Involved in Two Child Trafficking Cases," CECC China Human Rights and Rule of Law Update, 11. See also, CECC, 2006 Annual Report, 20 September 06, 100.

[27] Murray Scot Tanner and Eric Green, "Principals and Secret Agents: Central versus Local Control over Policing and Obstacles to 'Rule of Law' in China," 191 China Quarterly 644, 666 (2007).

[28] Ibid.

[29] U.S. Department of State, Trafficking in Persons Report—China, 80; "Vietnamese Police Arrests Three for Trafficking of Children to China," Agence France-Presse, 17 July 07 (Open Source Center, 17 July 07); "China, US agree To Enhance Coop on Global Issues," Xinhua (Online), 10 August 06.

[30] "ILO, China Join To Combat Trafficking in Children and Women," Xinhua, reprinted in China.org (Online), 12 July 03; International Organization for Migration (Online), "China Profile," July 2007; U.S. Department of State, Trafficking in Persons Interim Assessment—China.

[31] U.S. Department of State, Trafficking in Persons Interim Assessment—China; U.S. Department of State, Trafficking in Persons Report—China, 81.

[32] "Panel Set To Target Human Trafficking," China Daily. See also, "Ministry of Public Security Strengthens the Combating of Crimes of Trafficking in Women and Children," Xinhua.

Notes to Section II—North Korean Refugees

[1] CECC Staff Interviews; Joel Charney, "Acts of Betrayal: The Challenge of Protecting North Koreans in China," Refugees International, 12 May 05.

[2] International Crisis Group, Perilous Journey, Asia Report No. 122, 26 October 2006, 1.

[3] Department of State, 2007 Trafficking in Persons Report.

[4] Bureau of Democracy, Human Rights and Labor, U.S. Department of State, Country Reports on Human Rights Practices—2006, China (includes Tibet, Hong Kong, and Macau), 6 March 6, 07.

[5] Kim Young Jin, "Chinese Security Officer in Yenji Testifies, 'Increase in Arrests at the End of the Year,'" Daily NK, 1 February 1, 05.

[6] Kim Young Jin, "China Arrests, Shortly Repatriated to North Korea," Daily NK, 26 June 07; Donna M. Hughes, "How Can I Be Sold Like This?: The Trafficking of North Korean Women Refugees," National Review (Online), 19 July 05; International Crisis Group, "Perilous Journeys: The Plight of North Koreans in China and Beyond," Asia Report No. 122—26 October 06, 6; Ronald Schaefer, "The Forgotten Refugees," OhmyNews Web site, 9 October 06.

[7] Humanitarian workers assisting refugees have reported that many North Korean refugees attempt to reach Mongolia, and as a result China is constructing six new prisons in this region. See Charlotte Eager, "Korea's Oskar Schindler," Daily Mail, 30 June 07. On the construction of new facilities on China's North Korean border, see Melanie Kirkpatrick, "Let Them Go: China Should Open its Border to North Korean Refugees," Wall Street Journal (Online), 15 October 06.

[8] Convention Relating to the Status of Refugees, 28 July 51, United Nations Conference of Plenipotentiaries on the Status of Refugees and Stateless Persons convened under General Assembly resolution 429 (V) of 14 December 50, art. 33; China acceded to the Convention on September 24, 1982. "MFA Spokesman Calls North Korean in China 'Illegal Migrants' and 'Not Refugees'," CECC Virtual Academy (Online), 3 October 06.

[9] "Foreign Ministry Spokesman Qin Gang's Regular Press Conference on 19 June, 2007," PRC Ministry of Foreign Affairs Web site, 20 June 07.

[10] "Democratic People's Republic of Korea Ministry of State Security, People's Republic of China Ministry of Public Security, Mutual Cooperation Protocol for the Work of Maintaining National Security and Social Order in the Border Area," 12 August 1986, reprinted on the Rescue the North Korean People Urgent Action Network (RENK) Web site. According to James Seymour, RENK obtained and translated the document in December 2002. Seymour writes that "this document cannot be authenticated, but it does not seem implausible." On the 1998 agreement, see also Cho Kye-ch'ang, "Adds Article on Reinforcing Protection of a Special Train with Kim Jung-il on; Scope of Illegal Border-Crossing Expanded; Joint Countermeasures Included to Prepare Against Armed North Korean Escapees," Yonhap (Online), 22 January 07.

[11] James D. Seymour, "China: Background Paper on the Situation of North Koreans in China," Writenet, January 2005, 4–6.

[12] When China acceded to the Refugee Convention in 1982, it committed to honoring all provisions under the Convention and made only two reservations, neither of which is related to Article 33 on refoulement. Under Articles 26 and 42(2) of the Vienna Convention on the Law of Treaties, China's separate bilateral agreement with North Korea would not exempt it from compliance with its treaty obligations.

[13] Convention Relating to the Status of Refugees, art. 1.

[14] The United Nations Special Rapporteur on Human Rights in North Korea, "Question of the Violation of Human Rights and Fundamental Freedom in any Part of the World: Situation of Human Rights in the Democratic People's Republic of Korea," 10 January 05, 13.

[15] "Government Allows North Korean Refugees to Travel Directly to the United States," CECC Virtual Academy 28 August 06.

[16] Human Rights Watch, "North Korea: Harsher Policies Against Border-Crossers," March 2007, 7–8; Another source dates this tougher policy from 2005. Kwon Jeong Hyun, "10 Years of Defector Succession" Daily NK, 16 May 07.

[17] Human Rights Watch, 4–9.

[18] Norma Kang Muico, "An Absence of Choice: The Sexual Exploitation of North Korean Women in China," Anti-Slavery International, 2005.

[19] International Crisis Group, 18, citing David Hawk, "The Hidden Gulag: Exposing North Korea's Prison Camps," U.S. Committee for Human Rights in Korea, October 2003; Kim Rahn, "Female Inmates in North Face Compulsory Abortion," Korea Times, 29 September 06; Michael Sheridan, "On the Death or Freedom Trail with Kim's Starving Fugitives," Times Online (London), 3 December 06. Kwon Jeong Hyun, "10 Years of Defector Succession," Daily NK, 16 May 07.

[20] Stephen Haggard and Marcus Noland, "The North Korean Refugee Crisis: Human Rights and International Response," U.S. Committee for Human Rights in North Korea, 2006, 37–40.

[21] Haggard and Noland, 38–39.

[22] Haggard and Noland, 38; Convention Relating to the Status of Refugees, art. 35.

[23] Nicholas D. Kristof, "Escape from North Korea," New York Times (Online), 4 June 07; "China Imprisons N. Korean Defector Ring," Chosun Daily (Online) 28 May 07.

[24] "NK Refugee Supporter Released in China," Daily NK, 29 November 06.

[25] The State Council included the regulation on its 2006 Legislative Plan, and a January 2006 State Council General Office circular on the State Council's legislative work plan for the year listed the Ministry of Foreign Affairs, the Ministry of Public Security, and the Ministry of Civil Affairs as drafting Temporary Regulations on the Administration of Refugees. "Refugees Nearing Dream of Citizenship," People's Daily (Online), 1 June 07.

[26] "Refugees Nearing Dream of Citizenship" People's Daily.

[27] "Statement of the Media by United Nations High Commissioner for Refugees Antonio Guterres, on Conclusion of his Mission to the People's Republic of China," United Nations High Commissioner for Refugees, 23 March 06.

Notes to Section II—Freedom of Residence and Travel

[1] For a fieldwork-based case study that discusses the impact of the *hukou* system, including provisions allowing family members of urban *hukou* holders to transfer their status, see Dorothy J. Solinger, "The Sad Story of Zheng Erji Who Landed in the City Through the Favors Reform-Era Policies Bestowed But Rewrote the Rules While Suffering Wrongs, Once There," in Dorothy J. Solinger, ed., Narratives of the Chinese Economic Reforms (Lewiston, NY: The Edwin Mellen Press, 2005), 113–127, esp. 121, 123, 125.

[2] See, e.g., Universal Declaration of Human Rights (UDHR), adopted and proclaimed by General Assembly resolution 217A (III) of 10 December 48, art. 2, 13; International Covenant on Civil and Political Rights (ICCPR) , adopted by General Assembly resolution 2200A (XXI) of 16 December 66, entry into force 23 March 76, art. 2(1), 12(1), 12(3), 26; the International Covenant on Economic, Social, and Cultural Rights (ICESCR) adopted by General Assembly resolution 2200A (XXI) of 16 December 66, entry into force 3 January 76, art. 2(2). [See Section X, "Protection of Internationally Recognized Labor Rights," for more information on China's obligations

to comply with internationally recognized labor rights, include provisions relevant to migrant workers' status.]

[3] China is a party to the ICESCR and a signatory to the ICCPR . The Chinese government has committed itself to ratifying, and thus bringing its laws into conformity with, the ICCPR and reaffirmed its commitment as recently as April 13, 2006, in its application for membership in the UN Human Rights Council. China's top leaders have previously stated on three separate occasions that they are preparing for ratification of the ICCPR, including in a September 6, 2005, statement by Politburo member and State Councilor Luo Gan at the 22nd World Congress on Law, in statements by Chinese Premier Wen Jiabao during his May 2005 Europe tour, and in a January 27, 2004, speech by Chinese President Hu Jintao before the French National Assembly. As a signatory to the ICCPR, China is required under Article 18 of the Vienna Convention on the Law of Treaties, to which it is a party, "to refrain from acts which would defeat the object and purpose of a treaty" it has signed. Vienna Convention on the Law of Treaties, enacted 23 May 69, entry into force 27 January 80, art. 18.

[4] UN Committee on Economic, Social and Cultural Rights (CESCR), "UN Committee on Economic, Social and Cultural Rights: Concluding observations: People's Republic of China (including Hong Kong and Macao)" (Online via UNHCR Refword©)13 May 2005. E/C.12/1/Add.107, para. 15. This committee is charged with monitoring states' compliance with the ICESCR.

[5] State Council Notice on Endorsing the Public Security Bureau's Opinions on Promoting Reform of the Management System for Residence Permits in Small Towns and Cities [Guowuyuan pizhuan gong'anbu guanyu tuijin xiaochengzhen huji guanli zhidu gaige yijian de tongzhi], issued 30 March 01. Under these rules, migrants to small cities or towns may keep their land rights in their villages of origin. For more information on earlier reforms, see the CECC Topic Paper "China's Household Registration System: Sustained Reform Needed To Protect China's Rural Migrants," October 2005.

[6] See the CECC 2003 Annual Report for more information. CECC, 2003 Annual Report, 2 October 03, 52.

[7] Regulations on Legal Aid [Falü yuanzhu tiaoli], issued 21 July 03.

[8] State Council Office Circular on Improving Work on Management and Services for Migrant Workers in Cities [Guowuyuan bangongting guanyu zuohao nongmin jincheng wugong jiuye guanli he fuwu gongzuo de tongzhi], issued 5 January 03.

[9] State Council Circular Transmitting the Opinion of the Education and Other Ministries Relating to Further Work on Migrant Children's Compulsory Education [Guowuyuan bangongting zhuanfa jiaoyubu deng bumen guanyu jin yibu zuohao jincheng wugong jiuye nongmin zinü yiwu jiaoyu gongzuo yijian de tongzhi], issued 17 September 03.

[10] State Council Office Circular Regarding Work on Improving the Employment Situation for Migrants in Urban Areas [Guowuyuan bangongting guanyu jin yibu zuo hao gaishan nongmin jincheng jiuye huanjing gongzuo de tongzhi], issued 27 December 04.

[11] "Labor Ministry Officials Remove Regulatory Barrier to Migrants Seeking Work in Cities," CECC Virtual Academy, 4 October 06.

[12] Central Party Committee, State Council Opinion on Promoting the Construction of a New Socialist Countryside [Zhong-gong zhongyang guowuyuan guanyu tuijin shehuizhuyi xin nongcun jianshe de ruogan yijian], issued 31 December 05. See also "Communist Party, State Council Set Rural Reform Goals for 2006," CECC China Human Rights and Rule of Law Update, April 2006, 8.

[13] State Council Opinion on Resolving Migrant Worker Problems [Guowuyuan guanyu jiejue nongmingong wenti de ruogan yijian], issued 27 March 2006.

[14] PRC Compulsory Education Law, adopted 12 April 86, revised 29 June 06, art. 12; "Amended Compulsory Education Law Would Assure Migrant Children the Right To Attend School" ["Yiwu jiaoyufa" xiuding cao'an baozhang liudong renkou zinü shangxue], CCTV (Online), 1 May 06.

[15] Resolution Concerning the Question of Delegate Quotas and Elections for the 11th Session of the National People's Congress" [Guanyu shiyi jie quanguo renda daibiao ming'e he xuanju wenti de jueding], Guangdong News (Online), 16 March 07. "NPC's Approval of Key Laws Seen as Promotion of Social Justice by Chinese Academics," Xinhua News reprinted by BBC (Online), 16 March 07. Whether the resolution will give migrant workers a greater voice in practice remains unclear. In an article from the Xinhua news agency, one migrant worker expressed concern over election logistics since most migrant workers lack urban residence registrations, making them ineligible to vote in the cities where they reside. "Rural Migrant Workers To Enter China's Top Legislature," Xinhua (Online), 8 March 2007. In January 2006, the Shanghai local people's congress (LPC) for the first time allowed two migrant workers from Jiangsu province to attend a session of the Shanghai LPC as observers. The China Economic Times, a State Council-sponsored publication, criticized the Shanghai LPC, however, for not allowing the two migrants to serve as full representatives. It noted that *hukou* restrictions bar many migrants from standing for election, and that none of the 1,000 LPC delegates attending the session represented Shanghai's 4 million migrant workers. "State Council Newspaper Criticizes Lack of Migrant Representation in Shanghai LPC," CECC China Human Rights and Rule of Law Newsletter, March 2006, 13–14.

[16] "Hukou Reform Submitted To State Council, Legal and Fixed Place of Residence as Criteria for Shifting Hukou Registration" [Huji gaige wenjian bao guowuyuan, hefa guding zhusuo cheng qianyi tiaojian], Guangdong News (Online), 23 May 97. "Many Difficulties Remain in Hukou Reform, MPS Launches Investigation and Research into Legislating a Hukou Law [Huji gaige cun zhuduo nandian gong'anbu qidong hukoufa lifa diaoyan]," Legal Daily (Online), 20 June 07. There has been some dispute over the document's submission to the State Council. For background see Carl Minzner, "Hukou Reforms Under Consideration," Chinese Law and Politics Blog, 4 June 07.

[17] The current reforms bear close resemblance to earlier proposals put forth by central government officials. Nevertheless, one scholar has suggested that the current reforms are more liberal

than past efforts in that they only demand citizens meet a residence requirement, rather than both residence and income requirements, for transferring *hukou*. See Carl Minzner, "Hukou Reforms Under Consideration," Chinese Law and Politics Blog, 4 June 07.

[18] See Max Tuñón, "Internal Labour Migration in China: Features and Response," International Labour Organization (Online), April 2006, 10, 22–23, 35.

[19] For more information on local regulations that condition *hukou* transfers on meeting such criteria, see "China's Household Registration System: Sustained Reform Needed To Protect China's Rural Migrants," 4–5.

[20] Only certain types of rental housing qualify. The reforms permit other groups of migrants to obtain an urban *hukou* based on economic and educational criteria similarly used in other localities to restrict the number of migrants eligible to change their *hukou* status. Chengdu Municipal Party Committee, Chengdu City People's Government Opinion Concerning Deepening Residence Registration Reform and Reforming and Deepening the Integration of Cities and Towns (Trial) [Zhong-gong chengdu shiwei chengdushi renmin zhengfu guanyu shenhua huji zhidu gaige gaishen shenru tuijin cheng xiang yitihua de yijian (shixing)], issued 20 October 06, art. 2.

[21] "Shenzhen Municipal Authorities Announce Tighter Controls Over Migrant Population," CECC China Human Rights and Rule of Law Update, September 2005, 9–10.

[22] "Shenyang City Government Revokes Reforms to Temporary Residence Permit System," CECC China Human Rights and Rule of Law Update, February 2006, 9–10.

[23] "Beijing Eliminates Regulations on the Management of Migrants" [Beijing feizhi wailai renyuan guanli tiaoli], Beijing News (Online), 26 March 05.

[24] "Farmers Who Enter Cities and See a Doctor Can Be Reimbursed" [Nongmin jincheng kanbing ke xiangshou baoxiao], Beijing News (Online), 23 August 05.

[25] Ma Lie, "Xi'an District Grants Migrant Farmers Equal Treatment," China Daily (Online), 1 September 06 (Open Source Center, 1 September 06).

[26] "Chongqing High People's Court Issues Provisions, Traffic Accident Compensation To Be Carried Out According to 'Same Life, Same Value' [Principle]" [Chongqing gao yuan chutai guiding, chehuo peichang jiang zhixing "tongming tongjia"], Xinhua (Online), 19 October 06. A Chongqing court enforced this principle in December 2006 when it ordered that the parents of a child killed in a traffic accident be compensated at the rate for urban *hukou* holders, despite the fact that they were migrant workers with non-Chongqing *hukou* status. "'Same Life, Same Value' Ruling in Chongqing's First Urban-Rural Resident Car Accident Compensation Case" [Chongqing shouli chengxiang jumin chehuo peichang an 'tongming tongjia' panjue], Xinhua (Online), 13 December 06. For more information on compensation levels, see the CECC 2006 Annual Report, 20 September 06, 117, and "Lawyer Petitions for Constitutional Review of Discriminatory SPC Interpretation," CECC China Human Rights and Rule of Law Update, June 2006, 8–9.

[27] "Supreme People's Court To Release Determination on Issue of 'Same Life, Different Value' [Zui gao fayuan ni chutai xiangguan jueding jiejue "tongming bu tongjia" wenti], Xinhua (Online), 14 March 07. In 2003, the SPC issued a judicial interpretation mandating a lower rate of compensation for rural *hukou* holders. "Supreme People's Court's Judicial Interpretation Regarding Compensation Cases for Personal Injuries (2003)" [Zui gao renmin fayuan guanyu shenli renshen sunhai peichang anjian shiyong falü ruogan wenti de jieshi], Supreme People's Court (Online), 4 December 03, art. 29.

[28] State Council Office Circular on Improving Work on Management and Services for Migrant Workers in Cities [Guowuyuan bangongting guanyu zuohao nongmin jincheng wugong jiuye guanli he fuwu gongzuo de tongzhi], issued 5 January 03.

[29] "Number of Temporary Residents Nationwide is 86,730,000, Floating Population Needs Establishment of Socialization Management Model" [Quanguo dengji zanzhu renkou 8673 wan ren, liudong renkou ying jianli shehuihua guanli moshi], Legal Daily (Online), 26 October 05.

[30] Henan Provincial Party Committee and Government Circular on "A Program for the Construction of a Peaceful Henan" [Henan sheng wei sheng zhengfu guanyu "ping'an henan jianshe gangyao" de tongzhi], PRC Central Government (Online), 26 April 06.

[31] ICCPR, art. 12. General Comment 27 to this article states, "The refusal by a State to issue a passport or prolong its validity for a national residing abroad may deprive this person of the right to leave the country of residence and to travel elsewhere." Human Rights Committee, General Comment 27, Freedom of Movement (Art.12), U.N. Doc CCPR/C/21/Rev.1/Add.9 (1999), para. 9.

[32] PRC Law on Passports, adopted 29 April 06, art. 13(7). For an example of a beneficial provision within the law, see, e.g., Article 6, which stipulates time limits for officials to approve applications and allows applicants to contest rejected applications.

[33] Scholars and NGO staff have debated the legal bases surrounding the government's recent actions toward Yang. "Welcome Return for Chinese Dissident, Others Not Free To Travel," Dui Hua (Online), 27 August 07; Donald C. Clarke, "Yang Jianli and China's Passport Law," Chinese Law Prof Blog (Online), 28 August 07.

[34] "Yang Jianli's Application for Passport To Go to U.S. Still Has Not Been Approved" [Yang Jianli shenqing huzhao lijing fu mei reng wei bei pizhun], Radio Free Asia (Online), 15 June 07.

[35] See the CECC Political Prisoner Database for more information on Yang's case. Although initially charged with illegal entry, he was later charged with espionage for alleged connections with Taiwan.

[36] "Attorney Tang Jingling Brings Administrative Suit Against Customs for Taking His Passport and Preventing Him from Leaving the Country" [Tang Jingling lüshi dui haiguan kouliu huzhao zuzhi ta chuguo tiqi xingzheng susong], Chinese Human Rights Defenders (Online), 6 December 06.

[37] Claudia Blume, "International PEN Concerned About Writers' Freedom of Expression in China," Voice of America (Online), 6 February 07.

[38] Anita Chang, "China Bars Dissident's Wife From Leaving," Associated Press (Online), 11 June 07. "Zeng Jinyan and Yao Lifa Prevented from Leaving Country To Attend Human Rights Conference in Geneva" [Zeng Jinyan Yao Lifa bei jinzhi chujing dao Rineiwa chuxi guoji renquan huiyi], Radio Free Asia (Online), 11 June 07.

[39] "Mongolian Dissident's Passport Application Denied for 'Possible Harm to State Security and National Interests,'" Southern Mongolian Human Rights Information Center (Online), 8 August 07.

[40] "Persecution of Zheng Enchong Must Stop: HRIC," Human Rights in China (Online), 22 August 07.

[41] Maureen Fan, "Wife of Chinese Activist Detained at Beijing Airport, Authorities Forcibly Return Her to Home Village," Washington Post (Online), 25 August 07.

[42] "CAA Urges Chinese Government To Release Rights Lawyer Gao Zhisheng and his Family Members," China Aid Association (Online), 27 September 07. For more information on Gao, see the CECC Political Prisoner Database.

[43] "China Confiscates Muslims' Passports," Radio Free Asia (Online), 28 June 07. See also "Activist: Members of Muslim Minority Group in China Forced To Surrender Their Passports," Associated Press, reprinted in International Herald Tribune, 20 July 07.

[44] Yang Yingchun, "Ismail Tiliwaldi, While Speaking at an Autonomous Region-Wide Religion Work Meeting, Calls for Stronger Management Over Pilgrimage and the 'Two Religions' To Safeguard the Masses' Interest," Xinjiang Daily, 11 July 09 (Open Source Center, 13 July 07).

[45] "China Sentences Underground Pastor to 7.5 Years in Prison," Agence France Presse (Online), 8 July 06, reprinted on the China Aid Association Web site. See the CECC Political Prisoner Database for more information.

[46] "Two Priests Detained in Wenzhou After Arrest on Return from Europe," Union of Catholic Asian News (UCAN), 3 October 06; "Underground' Chinese Catholic Priests Charged, Likely To Face Trial," UCAN (Online), 26 October 06. "Two Underground Priests From Wenzhou Soon To Be Freed," AsiaNews, 17 May 07; "Two Underground Priests, Arrested After Pilgrimage, Sentenced Six Months After Arrest," UCAN (Online), 16 May 07. Authorities released Shao from prison in May to obtain medical treatment. "Jailed Wenzhou Priest Released Provisionally For Medical Treatment," UCAN, 30 May 07. Authorities released Jiang in August. "Second Of Two Jailed Wenzhou Priests Released, Diagnosed With Heart Conditions," UCAN, 29 August 07. See the CECC Political Prisoner Database for more information. Jiang Surang is also known by the name Jiang Sunian.

[47] Timothy Chow, "Chinese House Church Historian Denied ID Card," Compass Direct News (Online), 17 February 06, reprinted on the China Aid Association Web site.

○